a hands-on guide to the

Leland Atkinson

¡cocina!

techniques of southwestern cooking

PHOTOGRAPHY BY **Renée Comet**   FOREWORD BY **Mark Miller**

Ten Speed Press
Berkeley, California

For Lydia and Kenneth,
who taught me to chase my dreams.

A Kirsty Melville book

10

TEN SPEED PRESS
P.O. Box 7123
Berkeley, CA 94707

Distributed in Australia by E.J. Dwyer Pty Ltd; in Canada by Publishers Group West; in New Zealand by Tandem Press; in South Africa by Real Books; and in the United Kingdom and Europe by Airlift Books.

Text and cover design by Nancy Austin
Printed in Hong Kong

Library of Congress Cataloging in Publication Data
Atkinson, Leland.
  Cocina! : a hands-on guide to the techniques of southwestern cooking / by Leland Atkinson ; foreword by Mark Miller.
      p. cm.
  Includes index.
  ISBN 0-89815-841-9
  1. Cookery, American—Southwestern style. I. Title
TX715.2.S69A85 1996   96-12995
641.5979—dc20   CIP

1 2 3 4 5 — 99 98 97 96

words of thanks

Such a simple little book, yet so many talented and generous hands were needed to carry it to completion:

First, foremost and always, thanks to Mark Charles Miller for teaching me how these things are done, and for opening the door.

To John "Change of Address" Harrisson, the best agent and guidance counselor that a first-time cookbook author could hope for, for bouncing advice off of satellites from Pagosa Springs to Honolulu to Santa Fe, and for all of the reading, rereading, and gentle red corrections.

To Renée Comet, whose beautiful photographs give *¡cocina!* its soul. Thank you for your infinite patience and for lighting and composing chiles in a blender as carefully as the full-page shots. (Also for pretending not to mind as I wreaked utter havoc in the studio, leaving paint, sawdust, and achiote stains in my wake.)

To Renée's assistant, Ester "Where's the Fire Extinguisher?" del Rosario, who kept us organized and laughing, and also shirked her photographic and administrative duties to serve as the hand model for many of the "how-to's."

To Leslie Arnold, for remaining a far better friend than I deserve through all of this, and for all of the listening, pre-editing, and just being there.

To Chris Swinyard, Jay Comfort, and Doug Wilson, who saved me with recipe testing and development, and with advice on what to include and what to leave out.

To Red Sage executive chef Randell Warder, purchasing agent Scot Romoser, and to D. J. for help with food for the photographs. A very special thanks to the restaurant's entire staff for allowing me to create this in the eye of a remarkable tornado.

To Walter Scheib and the kitchen staff of the Casa Blanco for the support, advice, and a place to hang out.

To Olivia Cadavel, who trusted us with the beautiful Mexican cookware and plates that bring so much warmth to the photographs. Thanks also to Dean & Deluca, Pottery Barn, Williams-Sonoma, Kitchen Bazaar, and Santa Fe Style for additional props.

Thanks to Susan Dumont-Bentson of Cuisinart, and Hans Rothsach of Wüstof Trident Trading Co.

For chile bushes from some mysterious source in the middle of the blizzard of '96, thanks to Farmer Jones Produce. Also to Sally Harper of Del Valle Pecans in New Mexico for the last decent-looking branch of the year.

For literally lending a hand in the photographs and for helping with all of the details during shooting: Nathan McMackle, Nancy Walker, Margie Eyman, and Megan Cassidy.

Thanks to Kirsty Melville at Ten Speed Press for seeing a glimmer of potential in my awkwardly written proposal, and for taking a transcontinental leap of faith. Thanks also to Clancy Drake for editing and keeping everything on track and on time, Carolyn Miller for copyediting the manuscript, and to Nancy Austin for the beautiful design.

contents

foreword by Mark Miller

The first thing you should do when you start to cook southwestern food is get your mind in gear. Get your cowboy boots on (my old sharkskin boots always help me get into the spirit). This food is not namby-pamby, and the right mind-set is open, adventurous, and fun—the sometimes-staid rules and techniques of other cooking styles don't apply.

There are major differences in result when you don't use the right techniques: when I sample salsas with a strong smell of barely-cooked garlic, I know that the cook was working with an Italian mind-set. Garlic slow-roasted for an hour until sweet and creamy is very different from garlic sautéed in olive oil for ten minutes. Cooking a southwestern recipe in a stainless steel pot on an electric stove takes away the bold and complex flavors that originated with the use of seasoned cast iron and clay over the open fire. *¡cocina!* will show you, in easy steps, how to master the basic techniques that will make your southwestern food taste authentic.

Leland Atkinson worked with me at Red Sage for a number of years. He created wonderful masterpieces, always improvising and pushing the limits of traditional southwestern cuisine. But the final result always depended on his mastery of the essential steps that make the food what it is. He has compressed a lifetime of culinary experience into this small volume. I only wish this book had been available when I started to cook southwestern food.

In the late '60s, when I began my self-taught cooking course in Southwest Basics 101, I was prepared to leap into it. I had already experimented successfully with Moroccan, French, Italian, and Chinese cuisines, and I was confident that I was up to the new challenge. I loved this new world of interesting flavors and colors: fiery chiles called *ancho, guajillo, de árbol, pasilla*; rich, ripe, green avocados; fragrant cilantro; earthy fresh tortillas; woody, aromatic toasted cumin seeds.

There were very few good cookbooks on southwestern foods, and those few did not contain helpful instructions but were personal collections of recipes and anecdotes. I had watched my mother and others prepare marvelous southwestern foods, so I found that what I had to go on were my taste memories and my "kitchen common sense," both of which were in good supply. Still, my first attempts were very much trial and error.

My first try at making a chile sauce was a minor disaster. The chiles that the recipe called for were not available, so I went to the Latin market and asked what could be substituted. The chile I used was too hot and bitter. Later on, I found that chiles are often called different names in different regions; sometimes similar-looking chiles are called the same thing even though they are very different in taste; and stores often misname chiles. It's important that you learn the names, tastes, and appearance of the major chiles, fresh and dried. *¡cocina!*'s pictorial glossaries can help you; also, there are now good chile guide books and charts.

¡cocina! will take you from basic roasting, toasting, and grilling through recipes and techniques for classics like tamales, rellenos, enchiladas, and flans—all in one book. Leland's passion and precision are exactly the right blend for teaching about southwestern food, and he has chosen techniques and recipes that are the heart of the cuisine. If you can master these easy steps you will be able to cook some of the greatest food in the world, the food that is number one in my heart. I hope it will become a great passion in yours.

introduction

cocina *[koh-SEE-nah]* **n : kitchen**

scabeches, moles, tamales, rellenos: the truth is that, for most of us, this simply isn't the food our mothers taught us to cook. With all of the excitement that southwestern cuisine provides, its terms, methods, and ingredients can still be intimidating enough to scare a newcomer right out of the kitchen. And even though the aisles of most good grocery stores are now well stocked with the essentials, and new books on the subject are being published almost daily, the perception still exists that finding the ingredients, decoding the lingo, and using unfamiliar techniques will turn preparation into an all day affair.

But with roots that run 8,000 years deep, southwestern cooking is here to stay, and the time spent acquainting yourself with its methods, foods, and a little bit of its history will be very well rewarded. Through the diligence and inspiration of some very talented chefs, we have all discovered that to enjoy this rich blend of tradition and flavor means more than, say, just having a high threshold for spice. And knowing a little about the history and uses of the foods that are native to this continent seems to bring the flavors so much more to life.

This is an incredibly rich history: from the Pueblo Indians who grew corn, beans, and squash on majestic but challenging land; to the Spanish who carried with them a huge new range of foods that included pork, beef, and dairy products; to the Anglos who came down the Santa Fe Trail bringing the cultural diversity of their forebears and the secrets of their Dutch ovens; to the talented modern chefs have resurrected these marvelous flavors and brought them uptown.

The goal of *¡cocina!* is to celebrate the results of that history by showing you some of the things that make southwestern cooking unique, and to introduce you to a few of the touches that give this food its signature. Some of the techniques here are as ancient as the Native American practice of binding hearty sauces with toasted seeds and nuts. Others are as modern as a simple approach to range-top smoking. Hopefully, *¡cocina!* will allow you to bring the spirit and methods of some of the best southwestern kitchens into your home.

My only regret with *¡cocina!* is that we couldn't find a way to incorporate the marvelous aromas of these foods as they are being prepared: the only way to enjoy these sensuous pleasures yourself is to enter the kitchen and rustle the pots and pans (or the *comals* and *cazuelas*, as the case may be). If you enjoy this little journey through the pantry and past the hearth of the southwestern kitchen nearly as much as I have enjoyed laying the track for your travels, then you are in for a very special time indeed.

foods of the southwest

How many times has it been said? "I can't cook these recipes. I don't know what half these things are, and I'd *never* find all of the ingredients." One of the biggest stumbling blocks to learning Southwestern cuisine is the many unfamiliar ingredients. If you have never encountered or tasted huitlacoche, you will obviously approach a recipe calling for it with some trepidation. (Of course, some who *have* encountered huitlacoche will approach it in the same way, but that's another story.)

When it comes to locating the ingredients, most good grocery stores across the country now have aisles dedicated to Southwestern and Mexican ingredients. Corn husks, masa harina, and dried chiles and spices are all readily available in most markets. Even modest produce sections now carry four or five different types of fresh chiles. If for some reason your local market doesn't carry the basics, there is likely to be a Latino neighborhood not far from you, whose markets will better answer your needs. If neither of these options is viable, you will find some mail-order sources on page 131.

The next few pages are devoted to descriptions and pictures of the most commonly used ingredients, and more ingredients are discussed at the end of the book (pages 124–128). Of course, the foods of the Southwest are so vast in number that it would be impossible to discuss all of them in this book: there are over two hundred types of chiles alone, with new ones being discovered or hybridized all the time. Instead, we have chosen the foods that make up the foundation of this cuisine. Southwestern food at its best is powerful, dynamic, and explosive. It can be simple and straightforward or layered and complex, but with so many big, bold, and distinctive flavors, it is anything but understated. The foods on the following pages are a large part of the reason why.

chiles

Ancient South and Central American cultures knew full well what a prize they had in their coveted chiles. Not only did the fiery gems provide much-needed nutrients and add flavor and spice to their foods, they also served as cooling agents in a hot climate. The capsaicin contained in chiles invigorates the bloodstream by dilating the capillaries. This happy biological phenomenon improves the flow of both blood and perspiration, cooling you off even as your mouth lights up.

When Columbus "discovered" the New World, he became quite enamored with the chile. Believing that he had found a replacement for black pepper, which was at the time worth its weight in silver, he took the seeds back home with him. The chile quickly became so popular that within one hundred years it had circumnavigated the globe, invigorating the cuisine of every continent and island nation on which it landed.

fresh chiles

Fresh chiles add much more to other foods than just heat. From the Scotch bonnet, with its hints of papaya, mango, and tropical banana, to the buttery roasted poblano, to the grassy vegetable tones and bright tang of the serrano, heat is only a small part of the story. When using them, remember that the highest concentration of capsaicin, and subsequently the hottest part of the chile, is in the seeds and veins of the fruit. To tone down a recipe or a particularly hot batch of chiles, remove the seeds and veins before proceeding. If you are not used to working with chiles, wear rubber gloves when cleaning them. Take care not to touch your eyes or other sensitive flesh until you remove the gloves or wash your hands with lots of warm soapy water. The more you are exposed to chiles, the less they will irritate your skin (or your taste buds).

Because chiles begin to spoil from the inside out, they do not shelf ripen particularly well. A chile that spends 3 to 4 days on a warm shelf may look ripe outside, but when cut open, the interior may be black and slimy.

habanero

(ah-bah-NAIR-oh) Among the very hottest of chiles. Although the intense heat may make them difficult for some to appreciate, these chiles, along with their close cousins the Scotch bonnets, are perhaps the most flavorful of all the fresh chiles. Most cooks prefer to use these chiles in their ripe state, when they vary in color from yellow to orange to red. They have a wonderful tropical flavor that marries perfectly with fish and tropical fruit, and with tomatoes for salsas and sauces. Although they are often sold in their unripe green state, they are mellower (if something fifty times hotter than the jalapeño can be described as

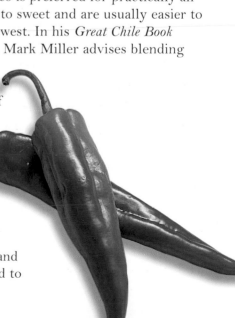

"mellow") and have a fruitier taste when ripe. These lantern-shaped chiles measure $1^1/_2$ to 2 inches long and are about $1^1/_2$ inches in diameter.

jalapeño

(hah-lah-PEN-yoh) Mild to medium heat. Jalapeños are the best known and most widely consumed chile in the United States. They are usually 2 to 3 inches long and 1 to $1^1/_2$ inches in diameter, with thick walls and meaty flesh. The jalapeño has a grassy vegetable flavor when green and becomes sweeter and milder as it ripens to bright red. The red jalapeño is dried and smoked to make the **chipotle chile**. Jalapeños can be diced with or without their seeds for salsas and marinades, pickled and sliced into strips or rings, and fire-roasted and peeled for blending into sauces or stuffed for cocktail-sized rellenos.

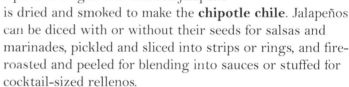

New Mexico green and Anaheim

Mild to moderate heat. Although, genetically, these chiles, also known as California chiles, differ only in the geographic regions in which they are grown, their characters differ dramatically. Hotter and cleaner in taste than the Anaheim, the New Mexico is preferred for practically all uses. Anaheims are mild to sweet and are usually easier to find outside of the Southwest. In his *Great Chile Book* (Ten Speed Press, 1991), Mark Miller advises blending roasted jalapeños with Anaheims to approximate the earthy punch of New Mexico chiles. Both chiles are 6 to 9 inches in length and 2 to 3 inches in diameter. Both chiles are usually roasted and peeled for sauces, salsas, and *rajas*, and the smaller ones are good to stuff for rellenos. Both chiles will ripen to a deep red color. They are usually strung into strings called *ristras* and hung to dry.

poblano

(*poh-BLAH-noh*) Mild to moderately hot. Deep green to almost black in the market, this chile ripens on the bush to a brick red color. When dried, it becomes the wonderfully earthy and versatile dried **ancho** chile, which is the most common of the dried varieties. Fresh poblanos are usually 4 to 5 inches long and 2 1/2 to 3 inches in diameter, tapering from their broad shoulders to a point. Poblanos are always roasted and peeled before being used in sauces and pestos or stuffed for rellenos. Fire-roasting gives them a wonderfully smoky character and buttery texture. Poblanos are the preferred and classic choice for making chiles rellenos.

Scotch bonnet

Extremely hot. Fruity and tropical in flavor, this chile is closely related to the habanero, and is often used interchangeably with it. Named because of their hatlike shape, these fiery chiles can be slightly sweeter than habaneros, with a hint of smoke. As with most extremely hot chiles, the seeds and veins are usually removed to tone them

down and to let their lush flavor come through. After preparing them, be sure to wash all knives and cutting boards well, lest you inadvertently spice up the next foods that you prepare. In the Caribbean islands and points south, experienced cooks shred the tips of Scotch bonnets below the potent seeds, and drag the chile through sauces and salsas and over the surface of meats and fish: this imparts a heady flavor without "lighting up" the dishes too much. Some wonderful bottled condiment sauces are made from these chiles; Busha Browne's Pukka Sauce and Coyote Cocina's Howlin' Hot Sauce are two of the best.

serrano

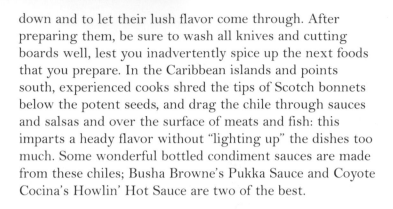

(*seh-RAH-noh*) Medium to high heat. One to 2 inches long and 1/2 to 3/4 inch in diameter and substantially hotter and more flavorful than the jalapeño, these little guys have a thick flesh and a hearty, bright vegetable taste with just a touch of citrus. Although serranos ripen to bright red, in this country they are almost always sold and used in their green state. The serrano is often chopped, puréed, or cut into fine rings with the seeds intact, as its pleasant heat is a major part of its charm. It is used in salsas, sauces, marinades, and escabeches.

dried chiles

If fresh chiles were sopranos, high and bright and clear, dried chiles would be basso profundos: deep and complex, as though drawn from the depths of the earth. As chiles dry, the flavors intensify and mellow as the sugars concentrate and the tannins develop. Different types of dried chiles are often blended together in a recipe to achieve a balanced complexity, just as different types of grapes are sometimes blended to perfect a particular wine. Indeed, descriptions of dried chile flavors can sound like critiques of fine wine: "Coffee, licorice, and plum, with a hint of tobacco at the finish." Dried chiles are indispensable in the southwestern kitchen, lending sauces and dishes a depth of character that is unattainable with any other ingredient. On these next few pages, the six most commonly used dried chiles are shown and discussed; more are discussed on page 125. Mark Miller's aforementioned *Great Chile Book* pictures and describes over eighty dried and fresh chiles and is a terrific reference guide for anyone interested in the genus *Capsicum.*

When shopping for dried chiles, look for fruits that are unbroken, flexible, and relatively dust free. Brittle chiles are either old or over-dried and, either way, will have lost a great deal of their precious flavor. With the exception of chipotles, which have been smoked, almost all dried chiles should have a light shine to their skins. Some cooks consider it to be unnecessary, but I recommend that you toast the chiles in a skillet or moderate oven to "wake up" the flavors before grinding them or adding them to a recipe. This technique is demonstrated on page 24. Depending on your heat tolerance level and the specific recipe, the seeds can be left in or discarded. However, when you are making purées or sauces that are to be strained, it is a good idea to remove the stems and seeds first to make the finished product go through a sieve more easily.

For purées, dried chiles are first toasted, then softened, either by boiling them briefly or by pouring very hot water over them and allowing them to stand, before they are puréed and strained. They are then in a convenient form for blending or adding to recipes. This technique is demonstrated on page 24–25.

ancho

(AHN-choh) Mild to medium hot. The poblano in its dried form is the most common of the dried chiles and also one of the best. In Spanish, *ancho* means "broad," and this wide chile is comparatively sweet, with hints of plum and raisin. Anchos are often blended with a few **de árbol** chiles to add some punch and to round out the flavor. Anchos make up one third of the "holy trinity" of chiles (the other two being **mulatos** and **pasillas**), which are blended together to prepare many traditional moles. Anchos are wrinkled and dark reddish brown in color, and measure about 5 inches long and 3 inches across the shoulders. They are most often used in sauces and stews, but are sometimes ground into a powder for use in chilis and spice rubs. When making sauces and marinades, try blending anchos with dried fruits or fresh stone fruits such as plums, peaches, and nectarines; adding a bit of molasses to complement and offset the spice; or flavoring the sauce or marinade with grassier herbs like thyme and marjoram.

cascabel

(KAS-kha-bel) Moderately hot. Literally translated, *cascabel* means "little rattler," and you can hear the seeds clatter around inside the brown sphere of the chile when it is shaken. Cascabels measure about $1^1/_2$ to 2 inches across and should have smooth skins. This excellent, woodsy chile has tones of tobacco, hazelnut, and citrus, and gives off a marvelous perfume when toasted. Use caution when toasting cascabels, as

their thin skins seem to burn more quickly than those of other types of chiles. Cascabels blend well with apples, pears, and other fruits, and with hard-bark spices like canela, cinnamon, and star anise. They are wonderful in soups, stews, and salsas, and they can even be used in salad dressings and vinaigrettes, where their nutty character blends beautifully with berries and vinegars.

chile de árbol

(deh AR-bohl) Spicy hot. These brick-red demons are very sharp and direct, with a slightly tannic, smoky flavor. They are tiny, about 2 to 3 inches long including the stem, and are light for their size. De árbols are hotter than hell, and their aficionados wouldn't dare try to tame them. They are often cooked and puréed with the seeds, and are best in sauces and marinades for beef or hearty game that can stand up to their substance. They also go well with citrus, tomatoes, and tomatillos, and with hearty herbs like rosemary and oregano. De árbols are often used to balance out and punch up milder chiles like anchos and cascabels.

chipotle

(chi-POHT-lay) Hot and smoky. Chipotles are dried jalapeños. Because jalapeños are thick fleshed and have a relatively high moisture content, they do not dry well. For this reason, the ripe red fruit is hot-smoked to accelerate the process. Probably the homeliest of the dried chiles, chipotles have little or no sheen and their skins are wrinkled and contorted. As a result of the smoking process, they tend to be a bit brittle compared to the leathery texture preferable in most dried chiles. Chipotles are by no means subtle: they are pure smoke and heat and impart a strong, woodsy flavor in very small quantities. Some cooks prefer the more complex *chipotles en adobo*—one of the few canned products that can be heartily recommended for cooking. Chipotles marry well with orange and other citrus flavors, balsamic and sherry vinegars, and bright fresh herbs like basil and cilantro.

guajillo

(gwah-HEE-yoh) Mild to moderately hot. These thin-skinned chiles are very resistant to being rehydrated and therefore will yield slightly less volume than other chiles when puréed. They are mild and slightly sweet, with soft berry and grass tones. Guajillos measure about 4 to 6 inches long and 1 to 1 $^1/_2$ inches across and are similar in appearance to dried New Mexico reds: guajillos have smoother skins and rounder shoulders. They are commonly used in soups, stews, and sauces, and their gentle compliant nature makes them a natural for chicken and pork dishes. These chiles pair well with blackberry and apple flavors and with softer, grassier herbs such as thyme and marjoram.

New Mexico red

Mild to medium hot. One of the few chiles to keep the same name in both fresh and dried forms, New Mexico red chiles are the base for the red sauces that play such an important role in Mexican and southwestern cooking. This relatively mild chile has a simple earthy flavor, slightly tart with a hint of dried cherry. New Mexicos are very similar in appearance to guajillos and share similar dimensions, but New Mexicos are slightly broader and more wrinkled than their smooth-skinned brethren. Although many types of chiles are strung in *ristras* for drying, New Mexicos are the variety most commonly seen hanging from the rafters of adobe dwellings in the Southwest and sold for decorative purposes.

herbs and spices

The spice rack of the southwestern kitchen benefited from the voyages of the Spanish and Portuguese. They brought cumin from the Middle East and coriander from the Orient. The seeds of both of these plants, and the fresh leaves of the latter (also known as cilantro), blended dynamically with chiles and other native foods. Canela, a more delicate form of cinnamon, was brought from Ceylon, adding its character to wild game, stews, and that most exciting of new concepts, dessert. These ingredients worked with native wild oregano and thyme, the more assertive epazote and herba santa, and a host of other indigenous plants to create one of the most satisfying and intriguing ranges of flavors in all the world's culinary traditions.

annatto seeds and achiote paste

(*ah-NHAT-oh*) and (*ah-she-OH-tay*) Although brick-red achiote paste is now more common, its source—the seed from the large and shady annatto tree—is still widely available. Achiote paste has a very pronounced earthy flavor, with a hint of iodine. It is prized as a coloring agent and is used commercially to color Cheddar cheeses and butter. Achiote is also used in slow-cooked sauces and stews, where it marries wonderfully with the flavors of dried chiles. It is very slow to dissolve, however, and needs to be ground. To make achiote paste from annatto seeds, soak them in water for at least 1 $^1/_2$ to 2 hours, drain them, and grind them in a spice grinder or blender. As the cooking liquid can permanently stain clothing (and the walls around your stove and blender), you may prefer to use achiote in the paste form. Tightly wrapped, it will keep for months at room temperature.

canela

(*ka-NE-lah*) Also known as **Ceylon cinnamon**, canela is lighter in color and more subtle in flavor than the cinnamon sold in the United States. Canela is the dried inner bark of the *Cinnamomum zeylanicum* tree, which was brought to Mexico from Sri Lanka. The hard, dark cinnamon sticks and ground spice more commonly sold in this country come from the *Cinnamomum cassia* tree. Because of its stronger, more pungent flavor and tougher texture, which makes it more difficult to grind, cinnamon is disdained by most Southwestern and Mexican purists. Canela is becoming increasingly easier to find outside the Southwest and is usually cheaper than cinnamon sticks. It has a rough, almost torn appearance, and its softer surface grinds easily in spice mills and blenders. If you cannot find canela, cinnamon is a begrudgingly acceptable substitute, but usually in quantities of $^1/_3$ to $^1/_2$ of the volume of canela called for in the recipe.

cilantro

Cilantro, the green leafy portion of the herb coriander, is used to brighten salsas, green moles, and pipiáns. It has a bright, clean taste that pairs well with spicy foods, and is often used in marinades and vinaigrettes. Cilantro also plays a vital part in Asian and Mediterranean cuisines and is thought to be the most widely used fresh herb in the world. In the market, it may be labeled as **Chinese parsley** or **fresh coriander**. Cilantro loses every ounce of its charm when dried and should be avoided; it's better to use fresh parsley and/or basil if cilantro is unavailable. It is best purchased during the spring and summer months, and it has substantially more flavor if purchased with the root base still attached. The leaves should be stripped from the thick stems and used either whole or coarsely chopped.

coriander

The dried round seeds of the coriander plant are fragrant and aromatic, with hints of lemon, sage, and caraway. These seeds have been found in Egyptian tombs and date back to at least 960 B.C. They are commonly used whole in pickling spices, or are toasted and ground for uses in dry rubs, soups, and salsas. Ground coriander is often paired with ground cumin to create an earthy blend of flavors that adds a distinctive character to Southwestern dishes and recipes.

cumin

Sometimes labeled under its Spanish name *comino*, this is another spice that was introduced to the Americas by settlers of Portuguese and Spanish origin. From a plant that is a member of the carrot family, cumin seeds are crescent shaped and resemble fuzzy caraway seeds. Originally used in Indian and Middle Eastern cuisines, cumin forms a perfect union with the equally earthy character of dried chiles and the slow-cooked flavors of the Southwest. As with most spices, it is best to toast and grind the whole seeds as needed. If only ground cumin is available, be sure to toast it slightly before using it to "wake up" the flavors and to give it a slightly nutty taste. As with caraway, some recipes for slow-cooked stews and fillings do call for the whole seeds.

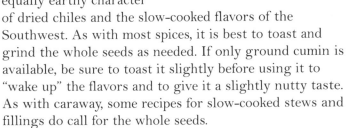

epazote

(eh-pah-ZOH-teh) Also known as **stinkweed**, **wormweed,** and the equally charming **pigweed**, epazote grows wild and until fairly recently was scorned as a weed in this country. The aroma from which epazote draws its colorful nicknames has been likened to kerosene, but the flavor is intense and unique, slightly reminiscent of eucalyptus. In Mexico, it is used to make a pungent tea and is cooked with all types of beans to reduce their gaseous qualities. It also plays a strong role in stews and soups, and brings a special untamed character to green pipiáns and moles. Epazote should always be cooked at least minimally to release its flavor, and the tender inner leaves are preferable. Fresh epazote is becoming more common in markets, but it is more often found in its dried form. Unfortunately, though dried epazote retains much of its wild flavor, the ratio of tough stems to tender leaves can be quite high. For this reason, it is best used in slow-cooked bean dishes or in sauces that will be strained.

hierba santa

(YER-bah SAN-tah) Literally translated, the name means "holy herb," and in Mexico it is thought to have many medicinal benefits, including the treatment of bronchial conditions. Often labeled as *hoja santa (OH-hah SAN-tah)* or *yerba santa (YER-bah SAN-tah)*, it contains flavors of licorice and sassafras. This broad flat leaf brings a special quality to green and yellow moles, and like most fresh herbs whose flavors are water based, benefits from being added during the last few moments of cooking. Although it is becoming more common in some markets, it can still be quite difficult to find. Try substituting equal parts fresh basil and tarragon, though you will need substantially less (about half as much by volume).

fruits and nuts

Before Spanish settlers planted plum and apricot orchards along the banks of the Rio Grande, fresh fruit was a rarity in the Southwest. Native Americans dried astringent wild chokecherries to mix into pemmican. They also cautiously peeled the fruit of the *Opuntia* cactus, which they valued more for its moist texture than for its slight sweetness. As the colonization of the New World progressed, the Chihuahua Trail provided a passageway for avocados, tomatoes, plantains, and other fruits from distant parts of the Americas, as well as a host of other exciting new foods that became part of a great post-Columbian culinary mix.

Nuts and seeds have long played a vital role in the region's native cuisine. Piñons were diligently extracted from pinecones and eaten out of hand or ground for thickening simple sauces and stews. Pepitas, the seeds from large squashes, were dried in the desert air and used in this way, too, giving pipiáns and moles much of their distinctive character. Pecans grew wild in southern New Mexico, and these members of the hickory family were cultivated by the European settlers along with their own highly prized almonds.

Here are descriptions of some of the southwestern kitchen's most commonly used fruits and nuts, and of cactus pads or nopales. Beans, which with corn and squash comprise a third of the "holy trinity" of southwestern food staples, are discussed on page 126.

banana leaves

Large and flat, banana leaves are ideal for wrapping fish for steaming and serve as a great alternative wrapper for tamales. They impart a wonderful tropical flavor to foods as they cook, and seal in moisture and flavors well. They are usually found frozen in Latin markets and better grocery stores, and should be toasted quickly over an open flame to awaken their natural aroma and flavor. If purchased fresh, the tough center ribs of the leaves must be cut away and discarded.

chayote

(cha-YOH-tay) Chayotes, a pre-Columbian squash, were a staple of the Mayan and Aztec cultures. Grown in Louisiana and marketed as *mirlitons*, they have traveled across the ocean to France, where they are sold as *christophenes*. This pear-shaped fruit has a smooth skin and a single large seed that is cut out after the chayote has been peeled and cut in half. Its crisp texture and mild flavor are similar to those of water chestnuts, zucchini, and cucumber. Chayotes can be scooped out and stuffed for baking, or julienned or diced for use as a side vegetable, a soup garnish, or an ingredient for salsas.

Although they can be used raw, chayotes are almost always blanched quickly to develop their somewhat shallow flavor and to brighten their color. They are most commonly available in the autumn or winter months.

cherimoya

(*chair-ah-MOY-ah*) Only recently becoming popular and available outside of the Southwest, the delicious cherimoya is also known as the **custard apple**. Originally cultivated in the mountains of Ecuador and Peru, it has an olive to gray rind when ripe, with an alligator-like skin. When cut open, it reveals black seeds and a fibrous but melting texture. When perfectly ripe, cherimoyas possess a rich and satisfying flavor heavily reminiscent of pineapple, mango, and banana, and sometimes a hint of strawberry. Their large seeds and fibrous texture make them a bit of a chore for eating out of hand. However, when seeded and puréed, they are wonderful in sauces, salad dressings, and sorbets. Cherimoyas are at their peak in December, but they are usually available through the early spring and sporadically throughout the summer.

nopales

(*noh-PAH-lays*) Nopales, or pads of the *Opuntia* cactus, are becoming increasingly popular and readily available outside of the Southwest. They can be cut into squares or strips and blanched for use in salsas or as a vegetable, or they can be pickled and served *en escabeche* (see page 38–39). Select fresh pads that are smooth and unwrinkled, and beware of the spines. Wear thick gloves when trimming them, a chore best accomplished with a sharp knife. Cut the pads into strips or diamonds and blanch them in two changes of salted boiling water. If you have tomatillo husks, add them to the water to eliminate the okralike sliminess that nopales can have. The crunchy cactus tastes slightly of green beans, okra, and asparagus, and is wonderful when marinated and grilled. Although nopales are readily available in cans and jars, these are products best left on the shelf. Purchase nopales during April and May, though they are available sporadically through the year.

pecans

The pecan is the most widely cultivated and harvested nut in North America. A member of the hickory family, which also includes walnuts, pecans grow in Mexico and in all southern states, and are vital to the economy of the Mesilla Valley in New Mexico. Containing more oil than almost any other nut (at least 70 percent) they were traditionally pressed whole to release the oil. Probably because of their pronounced flavor and high fat content, pecans are rarely used in moles and other nut-thickened sauces. Today, these nuts are used to add a savory crunch to meats, and to flavor salads and desserts. In the Southwest, the wood of the pecan tree is prized for cooking and grilling. It burns much slower than mesquite and provides more subtle tones than plain hickory. Pecans are harvested in the autumn months, and their high oil content makes them susceptible to rancidity. Store pecans tightly covered in the freezer.

pepitas

(*peh-PEE-tahs*) Often labeled as pumpkin seeds, pepitas are actually the hulled seeds from several varieties of large squash. For centuries, pepitas have been dried and toasted for eating out of hand and adding to other foods. Their relatively low fat content makes them a nutritious substitute for oily nuts such as piñons and pecans. Their green hue is only slightly diminished as the seeds roast, and they can add a colorful and low-calorie crunch to salads and pastas. Pipiáns, discussed on pages 28–29, are ancient sauces that use toasted pepitas almost exclusively for binding and to add a unique and distinctive character. Pepitas are also used to thicken and flavor many red and green moles.

piñons

(*peen-YOUGHNS*) Often labeled as **piñones**, **pine nuts**, or **pignoli**, piñons are seeds from the cones of several varieties of pine tree. All gathering and shelling is done by hand, and the shelling usually requires the cones to be heated. For these reasons, piñons are a fairly expensive commodity. They grow throughout the world, and in this country predominate in Arizona and New Mexico. They are also harvested extensively in Mexico, Italy, and North Africa, where they are incorporated into native dishes. Chinese pine nuts are exported to the States and are cheaper than the native species, but their strong pine flavor makes them less desirable for most dishes. If the label does not provide the country of origin, the less desirable Asian variety can be distinguished by its squat triangular shape, while native pine nuts are almost torpedo-shaped. Piñons are usually toasted, either in a pan on the stove, or in a moderate oven, but their high oil content and small size makes them susceptible to burning. The general rule is that if you can smell them roasting, it's too late. Piñons are used in both sweet and savory dishes and are ground to thicken pestos and moles.

plantains

Often referred to as **cooking bananas**, plantains have an almost squashlike flavor and are often fried when green or cooked and mashed like potatoes when ripe. Although very starchy when green, the flesh lightly sweetens and softens as the fruit ripens, and the

skins darken when ripe to an almost olive color with black streaks. Green plantains can be sliced thin and fried to make remarkable chips that are an addictive alternative to potato chips.

prickly pear

Coming from several varieties of the same cactus, including *Opuntia nopales*, the beautiful barrel-shaped prickly pear fruit has skin ranging in color from yellow to purplish red, and a deep scarlet interior. Mild in flavor, prickly pears have tones of watermelon and sour cherries. They lack tartness, however, and taste best when drizzled with a few drops of lime or lemon. Their taste may be "thin," and for this reason, prickly pears are often puréed and cooked down for use in sauces, vinaigrettes, and jellies. The Spanish settlers cooked them into a thick paste called *queso de tuna*, or prickly pear cheese. The skins of prickly pears contain spikes, which must be carefully removed by cutting off the ends and peeling the fruit, a task that is best performed while wearing gloves. The seeds are only slightly annoying when the fruit is eaten fresh, but for sorbets and other uses, the pulp should be puréed and strained. Prickly pears can usually be found at the market from September through December.

red bananas

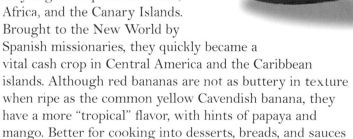

Bananas originated in India, and around the fourth century A.D. they began to spread to China, Africa, and the Canary Islands. Brought to the New World by Spanish missionaries, they quickly became a vital cash crop in Central America and the Caribbean islands. Although red bananas are not as buttery in texture when ripe as the common yellow Cavendish banana, they have a more "tropical" flavor, with hints of papaya and mango. Better for cooking into desserts, breads, and sauces than for eating out of hand, red bananas are fairly slow to ripen. They should be soft to the touch, with deep reddish brown skin, before being peeled for eating or cooking.

Roma tomato

Tomatoes were originally grown and cultivated in South America, but the tomato best suited for southwestern cooking was developed in Italy. Members of the nightshade family, tomatoes were thought by the early explorers to be poisonous, and the Europeans cultivated them strictly for ornamental purposes.

They slowly worked them into their cuisines along with the potatoes, corn, and squashes that were also unknown to them before the voyages of Columbus. The Roma, or **plum** tomato, was bred to have a higher ratio of flesh to seeds and watery placenta, and its firm texture makes it the preferred fruit for salsas, fire-roasting, and oven-drying. Its high ratio of surface area to total mass allows for quick blackening and yields sauces that are intense with tomato flavor without having to be reduced or cooked for long periods to develop their flavors. As with any tomato, Romas should not be refrigerated, which robs them of their flavor. Romas may be purchased year round, but are at their flavorful best during the summer months.

tamarind

(TAM-uh-rihnd) Occasionally labeled as **Indian dates**, the large brown pods of the tamarind tree were first used in India, Asia, and northern Africa. Tamarind pods have a brown papery outer skin that covers the sticky pulp, fibers, and seeds, and they bear a strong resemblance to bean pods. Brought to the New World by Spanish settlers, tamarind quickly took hold in Mexico and the Southwest. Its sweet and sour nature combines perfectly with dried chiles for sauces and glazes. Commercially, it is cooked into a syrup that is used to make a variety of popular soft drinks, and it is also one of the primary ingredients in both Worcestershire and Pick-a-Peppa sauces. Besides being sold in its fresh form, which is fairly labor-intensive to prepare, tamarind is sold in dried bricks with its seeds, as frozen pulp and purée, and as canned paste. A word of caution: many recipes calling for tamarind are not clear about which form is called for. Each type and brand has different concentrations of flavor and pulp, so add tamarind to your recipe gradually. The fresh pods can be purchased from late summer through early spring.

tomatillo

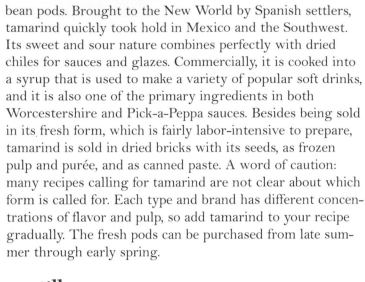

(toe-mah-TEE-yoh) A member of the nightshade family, the tomatillo resembles a small green tomato, except for the papery husk that reveals this fruit's kinship to the Cape gooseberry. Although tomatillos will ripen to yellow if allowed, they are usually sold, and are at their best, when bright green and firm inside their husks. Tomatillos have a sticky residue on their skins and should be washed in warm to hot water to remove it. This former staple of the Aztec diet tastes a bit like a mixture of green apple and lemon, and it takes on a faint herb flavor when cooked. Although tomatillos can be diced raw for salsas or puréed for sauces and dips, they are greatly enhanced by either fire- or dry-roasting, which allows the flavors to develop and deepen. Tomatillos are highly inconsistent fruits, with one batch being sweet and mild and the next being sour almost to the point of being inedible. As with tomatoes, it is sometimes necessary to add a touch of sugar to balance out the finished sauce or salsa. Although they are almost always available, tomatillos are at their best during the spring and summer months.

corn and corn products

(SEE ALSO PAGE 126).

corn

First bred by pre-Columbian civilizations from a wild grass around 5000 B.C., corn is one of the oldest of all cultivated plants. It played such a vital role in the lives of Incan and Mayan cultures that they incorporated it into elaborate religious ceremonies, naming it maize, or "our life." Today, there are over two hundred varieties of corn, and it is used for making everything from tamale wrappers and **masa harina** to biodegradable golf tees. Nonsweet **field corn** is the variety used to make **posole** and **masa.** This starchy corn is still preferred for the table in Mexico and South America, but the American sweet tooth has embraced several varieties of sweet yellow and white corn, both for cooking as a vegetable and incorporating into soups, stews, and salsas. **Sweet corn** is in peak season from May through September, and since its natural sugars begin their conversion to starch as soon as the plant is harvested, it should be cooked and eaten as soon as possible after it is purchased.

huitlacoche, cuitlacoche

(WHEAT-la-koh-che) In the rainy season, corn in the field can develop a fungus between the husks and the ripe kernels. Once affected, the kernels will blacken, contort, and swell to form this musty fungus that has been valued for centuries in Mexico. We know that the Aztecs possessed a sense of humor, because the literal translation of the word *huitlacoche* is "sleepy excrement." Unappetizing nomenclature aside, this food possesses an earthy and distinct taste that is faintly similar to mushrooms or truffles. It lends a black hue and resonant aroma to stuffings for empanadas, tamales, and quesadillas, and makes distinctive sauces. Huitlacoche is most often found in Latino and specialty markets and is usually sold cut from the cob and frozen. It needs cooking to release its wonderful flavor and lingering perfume, and it is often sautéed with roasted garlic and onions, and either fresh marjoram, oregano, or **epazote,** then simmered with a little water or stock. Huitlacoche is harvested during the rainy season, usually late spring to early fall.

posole, pozole

(poh-SOH-leh) Posole is corn that has been treated with slaked lime to remove the tough outer husks of the kernels, then dried. It can then be ground very finely into **masa harina** for use in tamales or corn tortillas, or ground coarsely for cooking into porridge or other grits-like dishes. Posole can also be boiled whole for hours to be softened for a traditional side dish or soups such as menudo, which is made with tripe, pigs' feet, or tongue. When cooked whole, posole is very similar in taste and appearance to the southern standard, hominy. **Chicos** are kernels that have been dried without the lime treatment, and subsequently have a milder flavor, but they can otherwise be used in the same manner. Finely ground chicos are labeled as **harinela,** which can be used interchangeably with **masa harina.**

tools you might need

You don't need a lot of exotic or expensive equipment in order to cook southwestern food. Chiles and spices were originally ground by hand with a *molcajete tejolte*, or mortar and pestle. A *metate* and a *mano*, or any elbow-shaped grinding stone and a pestle used like a rolling pin, were used to grind dried corn for fresh **masa** and **masa harina**, and large quantities of chiles for sauces. Yes, these labor-intensive procedures will help you get in touch with the true spirit of the Southwest as you duplicate centuries-old techniques for grinding ingredients and making sauces and masas. However, modern innovations such as spice or coffee grinders, food processors, and blenders allow us to achieve similar results in much less time.

In Mexico, foods are often cooked in colorful glazed earthenware pots called *cazuelas* and *ollas*. These vessels impart a wonderful and distinctly rustic flavor to stews and moles as they cook, but many of the glazes contain lead, which can be quite harmful. Unless they are clearly labeled as food-safe, avoid cooking in these beautiful vessels.

Here are some simple tools that are helpful for cooking southwestern food.

bamboo steamer baskets

Great for steaming tamales, these also make beautiful vessels for buffet service. Although they are not terribly durable, they are quite inexpensive. The 10- or 12-inch size is preferable. They are available in any Asian market and most good kitchen gadget stores.

blender

For puréeing rehydrated chiles and making sauces and moles. This is the preferred tool for making the smoothest possible purées and sauces, and for grinding large quantities of spices. Food processors accomplish many tasks almost as well.

candy and deep-fat thermometer

When frying rellenos and empanadas, or chiles for peeling, it is essential to have the oil at the right temperature. These inexpensive thermometers are available in most good grocery stores and kitchen-gadget shops for around five dollars, and the consistency that they will allow you to bring to your fried foods will make them more than worth the nominal investment.

cast-iron skillet

In Mexican cooking, a *comal*, or large earthenware or steel griddle, is the vessel of choice for browning meats, toasting chiles and spices, and cooking tortillas. They are not readily available in the United States, and the earthenware ones can break. A large, well-seasoned cast-iron skillet is a practical substitute for almost all southwestern recipes.

electric griddle

Definitely not essential, but the low even heat is ideal for browning quesadillas, requiring you to use less butter or oil than if cooking them in a skillet or sauté pan. An electric griddle is also good for warming tortillas and for keeping sauces warm. If you ever received one as a wedding gift, here's your chance to dust it off.

food processor

Ideal for the vegetable-based sauces, pipiáns, and moles of Southwestern cooking. The pulse function and broad base allows you to control the consistency of the finished product better than a blender does. It will not, however, grind chile purées and sauces as finely as a blender. With care, food processors can also be as useful for making doughs as a heavy-duty mixer. If you can only buy one piece of equipment, and the choice is between a blender, a mixer, or a food processor, choose the last.

mixer

A heavy-duty mixer fitted with paddle attachments is perfect for making dough for tamales and empanadas. Of course, they are also great for making breads and for countless other uses. Restaurants that make a lot of salsa fresca sometimes use the grinding attachment with large holes for chopping the vegetables.

mortar and pestle

Still ideal for grinding small quantities of chiles and for grinding garlic for aïoli. Beautiful large mortars can add the perfect touch to buffets when filled with colorful dips and salsas.

nonstick sauté pan or skillet

Great for dry-sautéing fish and poultry without added fats or oils. Fatty fish such as salmon require no oil at all, and even very lean fish and meats require the barest minimum. The high, prolonged heat necessary for dry-roasting, however, will eventually cause the coating to separate from the pan, so use a heavy skillet instead. The exception to this rule is pineapple, whose high sugar content makes it prone to sticking; it should therefore be dry-roasted in a nonstick pan.

propane torch

At first glance, this may seem to be the most frivolous item on the list, but a propane torch is good for fire-roasting tomatoes, peppers, and chiles. If your kitchen has an electric range, it is almost a necessity. The quick blast of heat is perfect for searing the skin without actually cooking the meat of the fruit. A torch is also handy for glazing the sugar crusts on crème brûlées, not to mention fixing those pesky leaks under the bathroom sink! The technique for using a torch for fire-roasting is shown on page 19. Although there are fancy models available with pistol grips, a basic propane torch can be bought in any hardware store for well under twenty dollars.

spice grinder/coffee grinder

To use for grinding dry chiles and spices. One of these can be purchased in any coffee shop or better food store for twelve to thirty dollars, and it is well worth the expense. The enhanced aroma and extra flavor of freshly ground spices are terrific rewards for the minimal effort required to produce them.

squeeze bottles

For applying cremas and streaks of colorful bean or fruit purées to plates and finished dishes. Squeeze bottles are a creative chef's best friend when it comes to applying decorative squiggles and zigzags. They are available from beauty supply shops and restaurant equipment companies. In a pinch, use recycled Gulden's or French's mustard bottles.

tart shells with removable bottoms

For making tamale tarts. Large ones, measuring 10 to 12 inches across, are ideal for a single tamale tart serving 6 to 8, and smaller ones, 4 to 5 inches across, are perfect for individual portions.

vegetable steamer

Ideal for steaming tamales. Although not as attractive as the bamboo steamer baskets discussed above, they are much more durable.

wire racks or grill screens

These are helpful for making jerkies, as they allow air to circulate adequately around the strips of meat as they dry. If you must, you can lay the meat directly on an oven rack, but cleanup can be a bit cumbersome. Racks and screens are also used for fire-roasting chiles and tomatoes over a gas flame, as well as for keeping fried foods such as rellenos and empanadas warm in a low oven. Resting such foods on paper towels can make them soggy on the bottom.

zester

Because many marinade and dessert recipes call for the zest of citrus fruits, this gadget is quite handy. If one is not available, the same result can be achieved by using a vegetable peeler. First remove the skin in strips, being careful not to remove the bitter white part, or pith, beneath the skin. These strips can then be cut into fine julienne.

before we begin

The recipes in this book are based on the following guidelines:

• Salt refers to kosher salt, which provides a clean, additive-free taste at moderate expense.

• All citrus juices are freshly squeezed.

• Butter refers to unsalted butter and olive oil refers to the virgin or pure variety.

• The heat levels of chiles vary widely from crop to crop. Keeping in mind that the line between pleasure and pain is personal, the recipes have been developed with the philosophy that eating should not hurt, and that chiles provide more of a flavor element than a source of perspiration. People with either exceptionally timid or asbestos-coated palettes should feel free to adjust the chile levels to their preference.

• Lard has played a vital role in the development of many of the dishes and recipes of the Southwest, and it adds a unique character to tamal and empanada doughs. However, the rendered pork fat has become such a taboo in our society that it has not been used in the development of any of the recipes for this book. Duck fat is called for in small quantities for refrying sauces, but corn or vegetable oils may be substituted.

techniques and recipes

fire-roasting and peeling chiles, peppers, tomatoes, and tomatillos

For countless centuries, the method for removing the bitter skins from chiles and tomatoes has remained unchanged. Native American and Mexican cooks roasted these foods over an open flame or, later, seared them on a very hot *comal* or griddle. The blackened skins of the tomatoes were then simply rubbed off with the fingers or a cloth, while the hot chiles were placed in earthenware vessels and covered with a cloth or animal skin. Once the trapped steam had cooked the chile slightly, the skins were scraped off and the seeds and pith were removed. Although neither the principle nor the basic methods have been altered over the years, we have found ways to achieve the same results without having to build a fire.

The fire-roasting and peeling of chiles and peppers not only allows their flavors to mellow and deepen, it also prevents the skin from coming off in unsightly sheets when the fruits are cooked in soups and sauces. In the Southwest, some chiles, including a portion of the New Mexico red crop, are roasted and peeled before they are hung to dry. They are then called *chiles pasados*, and the process results in chiles that are sweet and mild, with a slightly toasted, pleasantly complex flavor. Fire-roasting and peeling also make chiles intended for rellenos pliable and ready for stuffing.

When it comes to tomatoes and tomatillos, you may prefer to leave the blackened skins on and incorporate them into the sauces and salsas. They provide a smoky and woodsy flavor and look, and also serve to sweeten the dish slightly. The skins of chiles, on the other hand, tend to be bitter and are always peeled away after being fire-roasted. For home use and for blackening small quantities, the propane torch method may be preferable if you don't have a gas range. Not only does this procedure impress your friends, it is safe, more controlled, and makes cleanup a bit easier.

1. There are three methods for roasting fruits: over an open flame, under a propane torch, or in hot oil.

open-flame method: Place the food to be fire-roasted over the high open flame of a grill or gas range. Turn it as it blackens to ensure even roasting. A wire rack or screen can be laid over the flame and covered with the food to be fire-roasted. The rack will warp and darken with repeated uses. When working with small quantities, you may hold the food to be charred with tongs or impale it on a fork and sear it individually, although this is a rather inefficient use of time. Roast the food as quickly as possible, remembering that the goal is not to cook it but to blacken the surface and separate the skin from the meat. This procedure may also be done under the broiler of either a gas or electric range,

but the foods will lack a bit of the smokiness that comes from fire roasting. Although this method is easier, the foods tend to overcook before releasing their skins.

propane torch method: Place the food to be blackened in a cast-iron skillet or on another fireproof surface and light the torch. Adjust the flame to medium high and let the flame

make contact with the surface of the food. Move the torch over the surface, lingering no more than necessary to split and blacken the skin. Using tongs or a fork, flip and turn the food as needed to facilitate even blackening. Since the torch cooks so quickly, chiles, tomatillos, and tomatoes intended for sauces may need to be roasted in the oven very slightly after blackening and before proceeding.

hot-oil method for roasting chiles: If you have a bumper crop of chiles and need to peel them in a hurry, or if you seek a more delicate and less smoky flavor, sear the skins in hot oil. Use enough oil for the chiles to float without crowding. Heat the oil to about 375°, or almost smoking, and add the chiles carefully. Turn the chiles as needed and cook them

just until their skins are wrinkled, usually less than 1 minute. Drain them well, then cover and let them cool. Restaurants that use large amounts of roasted chiles sometimes use this method.

what not to do

1. **Don't overblacken the food. This will result in a dark, bitter sauce or a limp and overcooked food. The smokiness should be a pleasant byproduct of the process of separating the skin from the food that is being blackened.**

2. **Don't be afraid to turn up the heat. Using too low a flame will result in overcooking the foods. The beauty of fire-roasted tomato and tomatillo sauces is that they have been cooked just enough for the flavors to develop, but are still very fresh. Remember also that fire-roasted and peeled chiles should still retain as much of their texture as possible, and the more slowly you roast them, the softer they will be before releasing their skins.**

3. **If you are frying chiles to loosen the skins, don't overcook them. If the oil is hot, they should not require more than 1 minute of cooking. You can always cook them more, but a limp, mushy chile is a culinary tragedy.**

19

2. To peel fire-roasted chiles or peppers, put fruit in a bowl while they are still hot. Cover the bowl with plastic wrap or a heavy cloth. You may also cover the bowl with a plate or lid. Let the fruit cool for 4 to 5 minutes.

3. Remove the fruit and scrape away the skins with your fingers or a sharp knife. Avoid the temptation to rinse chiles, as this will wash away vital oils and, subsequently, flavor.

4. To cut chiles into *rajas* (thin strips), or if you plan to dice or purée chiles or peppers, split them open and drain away the liquid and seeds. Trim the stem and pointed ends and lay the chile or pepper flat. Trim away the ribs and any attached seeds and discard them. The chile or pepper is now ready for cutting into the desired form. The preparation of chiles for rellenos is illustrated on pages 61–62.

what not to do

1. **Don't soak chiles or peppers in water. Yes, this will make them easier to peel, but they will lose much of their flavor and take on the texture of a wet tissue. Try wiping them with a paper towel or cooking them a bit more. If you absolutely must, rinse them very briefly under running water.**

2. **If you are having trouble peeling chiles or peppers, either they were not cooked enough, or they were not wrapped tightly after roasting. Here's your chance to try out the new propane torch for a little "spot roasting."**

fire-roasted tomato and scotch bonnet salsa

makes about 2 cups

This is a wonderful sauce for empanadas and grilled meats, and it is even good as a dip with old corn tortillas. Fussy cooks might wipe away the charred skins before puréeing to yield a perfectly red sauce, but leaving them in provides a more rustic look and a smoky flavor. Fire-roasting Scotch bonnets develops their full tropical flavor, but it also unleashes all of the fiery potential of this exciting chile. Cooks who are preparing for a crowd with timid palates are advised to add the chiles in smaller quantities or to use jalapeños instead. For a cooler alternative to the tropical flavor note of Scotch bonnets, substitute smoky chipotle purée for the fresh chiles.

Fire-roasted, or blackened, sauces are beautiful when spooned out on plates, but they can separate, or "weep," after a few moments. Although some cooks prefer to reduce them to prevent this from occurring, this can destroy the beautiful fresh flavor that makes these sauces unique. Try binding them with cornstarch as in this recipe, but remember not to cook the sauces any longer than necessary to just thicken them.

3 teaspoons olive oil

$^1/_2$ large onion, sliced

12 Roma tomatoes (about 1 $^1/_2$ pounds), fire-roasted (see pages 18–19)

2 to 3 Scotch bonnet chiles, fire-roasted (see pages 18–19) and seeded but not peeled, or 2 tablespoons Chipotles en Adobe Purée (page 26)

1 $^1/_2$ teaspoons kosher salt or to taste

Juice of 2 limes

1 teaspoon sugar or as needed

1 tablespoon cornstarch mixed with 1 $^1/_2$ tablespoons water (optional)

In a medium sauté pan or skillet over medium-high heat, heat 2 teaspoons of the oil and sauté the onion for 4 to 8 minutes, or until golden brown and completely soft. Set aside.

Put the onion, tomatoes, chiles, and salt in a blender or food processor and purée until the desired consistency is achieved. For a dipping salsa, leave the mixture rather chunky. To serve as a sauce for plated food, purée it until it is smooth, adding a little water as needed to thin. Add the remaining 1 teaspoon oil, the lime juice, and sugar. Taste and adjust the seasoning.

To bind the sauce, put it in a medium saucepan and bring it to a gentle simmer. Stir the cornstarch mixture and pour a few drops of it into the sauce. Continue adding the cornstarch mixture in small amounts until the desired thickness is achieved. The sauce should be served just slightly warmer than room temperature.

chile seco salsa

makes about 3 cups

The harmony between the bright freshness of tomatoes, the deep tones of dried chiles, and the sweet-tart taste of orange is very satisfying in this simple sauce. It goes well with grilled meats, especially lamb, and is a wonderful dipping sauce for Pork Carnitas Empanadas (page 70). This salsa goes well with tamales and rellenos, too, and is super-easy to make. To make the sauce less hot, use chipotle purée in place of Scotch bonnets in the tomato sauce.

1 *each* large ancho chile, guajillo chile, and dried New Mexico red chile, seeded and toasted (see page 24)

1 cup orange juice

2 cups Fire-Roasted Tomato and Scotch Bonnet Salsa (page 21)

Fresh lime juice to taste

Salt to taste

Put the chiles in a medium saucepan with the orange juice and bring it to a simmer. Cook the mixture for 3 to 5 minutes, or until the chiles have softened completely and the juice has reduced by one third. Add the salsa and bring it to a boil. Transfer the sauce to a blender or food processor and purée it until quite smooth. For a more saucelike consistency, add a little water as needed. Add the lime juice and salt. Taste and adjust the seasoning. Serve warm or hot. Store in an airtight container in the refrigerator for up to 3 days.

Fire-Roasted Tomatillo Salsa with Basil (top), Chile Seco Salsa (middle), Fire-Roasted Tomato and Scotch Bonnet Salsa (bottom)

fire-roasted tomatillo salsa with basil

makes about 2 cups

Tomatillos are a vital ingredient in Mexican and southwestern cooking, where their tart apple-citrus qualities marry perfectly with fresh chiles, cilantro, and other fresh herbs in many classic green sauces and moles. In this sauce, the chipotles add a light reddish-brown color and smoky touch that is interesting against the slight licorice tones of the basil. Serve this sauce with chips, tamales, and grilled meats and seafood.

3 $^1/_2$ teaspoons olive oil

$^1/_2$ cup sliced onion

15 tomatillos (about 1 $^1/_2$ pounds), soaked in warm water for 30 minutes, husked, and fire-roasted (see pages 18–19)

1 tablespoon Chipotles en Adobo Purée (page 126)

$^1/_2$ teaspoon salt or to taste

$^1/_2$ teaspoon sugar or to taste

Juice of 1 large lime

$^1/_2$ cup fresh basil leaves, coarsely chopped

In a medium sauté pan or skillet over medium-high heat, heat 2 teaspoons of the oil and sauté the onion, stirring occasionally, for 4 to 8 minutes, or until golden brown and completely soft. Place the tomatillos, onion, and chipotle purée in a blender or food processor and pulse to a coarse or smooth purée, as you prefer, adding a little water to thin as necessary. Add the salt, sugar, and lime juice. Taste and adjust the seasoning. Stir in the chopped basil and let sit at room temperature for 1 hour before serving. Store in an airtight container in the refrigerator for up to 3 days. Taste and adjust the seasoning of the chilled sauce, and thin it with a little water, if necessary.

rehydrating and puréeing dried chiles

Any recipe that contains chiles should receive the disclaimer "more or less to taste." Because climate, rainfall, and levels of sunlight can contribute to the amount of capsaicin in the chile, no two batches will have quite the same level of fire. That is why your favorite dish in a southwestern restaurant may be mild on one visit, but smokin' the next. One cup of chiles is always 1 cup of chiles, but sometimes that can be too much. The easiest way to control the heat, flavor, and color of dishes containing dried chiles is to make them into purées. They may then be added to dishes in increments to achieve the desired balance of heat and flavor. These purées have a long shelf life and make a convenient addition to your pantry.

1. If the chiles are dirty or dusty, wipe them with a dry cloth. Next, stem and seed them by breaking off the stem and either breaking open the chile or cutting it open with scissors. Seed smaller chiles such as de árbols by breaking off the stems and rolling the chiles back and forth in your hands. You won't remove all of the seeds, but this purée is prized for its heat. For a hotter purée, process the chiles *with* the seeds.

2. Dried chiles may be toasted on the stovetop or in the oven. As dried chiles are expensive and their low moisture content allows them to burn at low temperatures, it is safer to toast them in the oven. Preheat the oven to 250°. Put the chiles in a dry cast-iron skillet and toast them in the oven for 1 to 2 minutes, or until they darken slightly and release their perfume. If you choose to toast them on the stovetop, do so over moderate heat for 1 or 2 minutes, and watch the chiles carefully to keep them from burning.

3. Place the toasted chiles in a saucepan and cover them with hot or boiling water. Weight them with a small plate to keep them submerged and let them sit for 30 to 40 minutes, or until soft.

microwave method

Put the stemmed and seeded chiles in a microwavable bowl and pour in water to cover. Wrap the bowl tightly with plastic wrap and place it in the microwave. Cook the chiles on high for 2 to 3 minutes. Remove the bowl from the oven and allow it to sit for 3 to 5 minutes, or until the chiles have cooled slightly. Watch out for dangerous steam when unwrapping the bowl.

4. Transfer the chiles to a blender or food processor. Taste the soaking water. If it is not bitter, add just enough of it to facilitate a smooth purée. If it is bitter, substitute fresh water instead. Purée the chiles until smooth.

5. Using a spoon or spatula, force the purée through a medium-fine strainer. Store in an airtight container in the refrigerator for up to 8 days, or freeze for up to 6 months. Chipotles en adobo purée will keep much longer.

what not to do

1. Be careful not to scorch or burn the chiles when toasting them, or they will yield an acrid and bitter purée.

2. Add enough of the soaking liquid to make a smooth purée.

chipotles en adobo

makes 1 ¹/₄ cups

The chipotle, or smoked jalapeño, is a very direct and powerful chile that is often prized more for its smoke and heat than for any nuances of subtle flavor. Adding the ingredients listed below "mellows" the chipotles a bit and gives them a nice complexity that complements many other foods. The vinegar and ketchup will also extend the shelf life of the chiles. For convenience, canned chipotles en adobo make an excellent substitute.

1 packed cup (2 ounces) stemmed chipotle chiles

2 tablespoons finely chopped onion

4 tablespoons ketchup

1 teaspoon minced garlic

¹/₄ cup cider vinegar

3 cups water

¹/₂ teaspoon salt

Put all the ingredients in a medium nonreactive saucepan over medium heat and bring the liquid to a simmer. Cover and cook for about 15 minutes. Uncover and continue to cook for 45 minutes, or until a saucelike consistency is achieved.

To make in a microwave, reduce the amount of water to 1 ¹/₄ cups and place all ingredients in a microwavable bowl and seal well with plastic wrap. Cook the mixture on high power for 2 to 3 minutes and allow it to sit for 3 to 5 minutes. Watch out for the steam when uncovering the bowl.

Let cool. Store in an airtight container in the refrigerator for up to 3 weeks.

CHIPOTLES EN ADOBO PURÉE: Transfer the chiles and their sauce to a blender or food processor and blend to a smooth purée. Strain through a medium-meshed strainer. Let cool. Store in an airtight container in the refrigerator for up to 3 weeks. Makes 1 cup.

dried chile purées

makes 1 cup purée

Having these purées on hand can cut down on your time in the kitchen and can help you to more accurately control the heat level of your finished sauces and other dishes. What follows are guidelines for the chiles most commonly used for purées, with counts and proportions. Remember that dried chiles do not benefit from extended cooking, so add purée to sauces and stews towards the end of their time on the stove. Since the shape and size of all blenders are different, the amount of soaking liquid or water needed to purée the chiles will vary; use just enough to yield a smooth purée. The technique for rehydrating and puréeing chiles are discussed on page 24.

chiles de árbol and cider vinegar purée

makes 1 cup

Like the chipotle chile, de árbols are about as subtle as a high-speed locomotive. Since they are often used to spice up dishes where more complex chiles predominate, you may want to leave the seeds in and use them full force. Using straight vinegar instead of water gives the purée an extended shelf life as well as flavor, and a little of it goes a long way indeed.

1 cup (about 1 ounce) chiles de árbol, stemmed

1 1/2 cups cider vinegar

2 tablespoons finely chopped onion

1 tablespoon minced garlic

For a milder purée, rub the chiles between your palms to remove most of the seeds. Chop the chiles coarsely with a knife or in a food processor. Put them in a medium bowl and pour the vinegar over. Cover and refrigerate overnight.

Add the onion and the garlic to the chiles and either cover the bowl with plastic and microwave on high for 1 minute, or put them in a medium saucepan over medium-high heat, cover, and simmer for 3 minutes. Let cool slightly, then purée in a blender until very smooth. Let cool. Store in an airtight container for up to 1 month.

Chile	Number	Weight (seeds & stems removed)	Volume	Water to Rehydrate
ancho	5 to 7	2 ounces	1 1/2 cups	1 1/2 cups
cascabel	25 to 30	2 1/2 ounces	1 1/2 cups packed	1 1/3 cups
guajillo	15 to 20	2 1/4 ounces	1 1/2 cups	1 1/2 cups
New Mexico red	8 to 10	1 1/2 ounces	1 1/2 cups	1 1/3 cups

Ancho Purée (top), Chile de Árbol Purée (middle), and New Mexico Red Chile Purée (bottom)

pipiáns and moles

Native Americans have been binding their rustic sauces with ground nuts, seeds, and dried corn for ages untold. When Cortés dined with the Aztec emperor Montezuma, he was served pipián rojo, a red sauce thickened with ground toasted pepitas and dried chiles.

To vastly oversimplify the difference between pipiáns and moles *(MOH-lays)*, pipiáns are bound primarily with pepitas, while most but not all moles are thickened with a variety of seeds and nuts. Pipiáns can be thicker than moles, and they are sometimes used in much the same manner as pestos. Moles are much more elaborate, and were originally developed to showcase the affluence of the hosts who were serving them. The misconception that moles are chocolate-based sauces stems from the fact that mole poblano and other dark moles use a touch of the sweet ingredient to offset the slight bitterness that can come from toasting the seeds, nuts, and chiles.

Although recipes will vary slightly from source to source, there are two basic pipiáns: red, or *rojo*, and green, or *verde*. Each region of Mexico produces at least one version of mole, and the town of Oaxaca is known as the Land of the Seven Moles, some of which are extremely complex. Some recipes for moles can have a list of ingredients that run a full two pages, calling for a cornucopia of dried chiles, nuts, seeds, and spices.

For the sake of clarity, I have chosen to illustrate the preparation of a relatively simple pipián rojo:

1. Stem, seed, and toast the chiles (see page 24). Put them in a medium bowl, cover them with hot water, weight them with a small plate, and soak for 20 minutes or until soft.

2. Toast the pumpkin seeds (see page 117).

3. Fire-roast the tomatoes (see pages 18–19), and sauté the onion until browned and soft, 3 to 5 minutes. Put the tomatoes, onions, and pumpkin seeds in a blender or food processor and purée them to a paste.

Add the chiles and all the remaining ingredients (except the stock and fat) and purée, adding stock as necessary to make a smooth sauce.

4. In a large sauté pan or wide saucepan over medium-high heat, heat the duck fat or vegetable oil until it is almost smoking. Pour the pipián into the pan, being careful to avoid the spattering, and fry it for 3 to 5 minutes, stirring constantly. Let the sauce cool to room temperature and serve.

what not to do

1. As always, avoid scorching or overtoasting the chiles and nuts, which will make the sauce bitter.

2. Don't omit the frying step. Although it can be messy, and can cause green moles and pipiáns to lose some of their vibrant color, it is a vital step in the melding of the different flavor elements.

pipián rojo

makes about 4 cups

Pipiáns can be made to be as thick as pestos and slathered over roasted or grilled meats and poultry, or they can be brothy to the point of being served as a soup with cooked chicken and lime wedges. This recipe falls somewhere in between, with the optional duck or chicken stock giving the pipián a nice saucelike consistency. It is perfect to serve with roasted fowl, especially duck. To make a thicker pipián, simply use less stock or soaking water from the chiles.

Four 1-inch sticks of canela, or two 1-inch sticks of cinnamon

$^1/_2$ teaspoon whole allspice

2 *each* ancho and guajillo chiles, stemmed, seeded, and toasted (see page 24)

2 teaspoons olive oil

4 Roma tomatoes, fire-roasted (see pages 18–19)

$^1/_2$ onion, diced

1 cup pepitas, toasted (see page 117)

2 Chipotles en Adobo (page 25)

1 teaspoon adobo sauce

1 $^1/_2$ teaspoons salt or to taste

1 teaspoon sugar or to taste

$^1/_2$ cup unsalted roasted peanuts

1 to 2 cups duck or chicken stock or soaking water from the chiles

1 teaspoon rendered duck fat or vegetable oil

Grind the canela and allspice berries in a spice grinder. Set aside. Put the chiles in a medium bowl, cover them with hot water, weight them with a small plate, and soak them for 20 minutes.

In a small sauté pan or skillet over medium-high heat, heat the olive oil and sauté the onion until it is browned and

soft, 3 to 5 minutes. Put the tomatoes, onion, and pepitas in a blender or food processor and purée to a paste. Add the chiles and all the remaining ingredients except the stock and duck fat, and purée, adding stock as necessary to make a smooth sauce.

In a large sauté pan or wide saucepan over medium-high heat, heat the duck fat until it is almost smoking. Pour the sauce into the pan, being careful to avoid the spattering, and fry it for 3 to 5 minutes, stirring constantly. Let cool to room temperature and serve.

pipián verde

makes about 4 cups

While pipián rojo uses dried chiles for color and deep, reso-nant flavors, this recipe relies on fresh chiles and bright green ingredients, with toasted pepitas balancing it out. This recipe yields a sauce that complements grilled fish, scallops, and chicken. For a more pestolike topping that can be slathered or mounded over the top of grilled meats and seafoods, simply reduce the amount of chicken stock.

8 leaves romaine lettuce, trimmed and coarsely chopped

8 large (6 ounces) tomatillos, soaked in warm water for 30 minutes and husked

2 large hierba santa leaves or young avocado leaves, chopped, or $^1/_2$ cup fresh cilantro leaves

1 $^1/_2$ packed cups watercress leaves or radish tops (about 1 bunch)

$^1/_2$ cup fresh cilantro leaves (about $^1/_2$ bunch)

2 to 4 serrano chiles, coarsely chopped

3 cloves garlic, dry-roasted (see page 116)

$^1/_2$ cup finely diced onion

1 teaspoon cumin seeds, toasted (see page 117)

1 to 1 $^1/_2$ cups chicken stock

1 cup (4 ounces) pepitas, toasted (see page 117)

1 teaspoon salt or to taste

Freshly ground black pepper to taste

1 teaspoon sugar or to taste (optional)

2 tablespoons rendered duck fat or vegetable oil

Put the romaine, tomatillos, herbs, 2 of the serranos, garlic, onion, and cumin in a blender. Pour in 1 cup of stock and the pepitas and process until smooth. Taste to see if more serranos are needed. Add the salt, pepper, sugar, and additional serranos if desired; purée. Adjust the thickness of the pipián with more chicken stock, as desired.

In a large sauté pan or wide saucepan over medium heat, heat the duck fat until it is almost smoking. Pour the pipián carefully into the hot pan and fry for 3 to 6 minutes, stirring occasionally. Serve the sauce slightly warmer than room tem-perature, but do not overheat it or keep it warm for longer than 1 or 2 hours.

Pipian Rojo (back left), Pueblo Mole being prepared (bottom)

pueblo mole

makes about 4 cups

Legend has it that mole poblano, or the rich, dark mole that is one of the most famous of all Mexican dishes, was created in the late 1600s as a tribute to the viceroy of New Spain. That mole, complex and rich with myriad chiles, chocolate, nuts, and spices, contains as many as thirty ingredients, highlighting the bounty of the region. The mole recipe below stays true to that spirit, but limits your grocery list by quite a few ingredients. Serve it with roasted turkey or duck, or grilled chicken, quail, or rabbit. To provide a sharp foil for the savory sauce, serve this with a bowl of lime wedges.

Four 1-inch pieces of canela, or two 1-inch pieces
　　of cinnamon

1 scant teaspoon whole fresh allspice

1 to 2 ancho chiles, 3 to 4 guajillo chiles, and 3 to
　　4 dried New Mexico red chiles, stemmed, seeded,
　　and toasted (see page 24)

$^1/_2$ cup *each* piñons, pepitas, and pistachios, toasted
　　(see page 117)

$^1/_2$ cup Grilled Onion (page 51), or $^1/_2$ cup Caramelized
　　Onion (page 51)

2 to 3 Roma tomatoes, fire-roasted (see pages 18–19)

5 large cloves garlic, dry-roasted (see page 116)

1 sprig fresh thyme

1 teaspoon dried Mexican oregano

$1^1/_2$ teaspoons achiote paste (optional)

4 cups chicken stock (page 122)

$^1/_3$ teaspoon salt or to taste

2 ounces semisweet chocolate, chopped

Juice of 2 limes or to taste

Grind the canela and allspice in a spice grinder. Put the ground spices and all of the remaining ingredients except the chocolate and lime juice in a large saucepan and bring to a boil. Immediately reduce the heat to a simmer and cook for 15 to 20 minutes. Remove from heat. Remove and discard the thyme sprig. Let the mixture cool slightly.

Transfer the mixture to a blender, add the chocolate, and purée until it is smooth, in 2 batches if necessary. Strain the mole though a medium-meshed sieve. Add the lime juice. Taste and adjust the seasoning. Serve slightly warmer than room temperature.

salsas

If sauces were a symphony, then salsas would be a mariachi band: brash and loud and full of spirit. A good salsa bombards the senses and adds a vibrant note to other foods. Fresh salsa can render boring foods electric, and sweet and tart fruit-based salsas can soothe the fire of spicier dishes. The range of salsa possibilities is endless, and the shelves of bookstores are rapidly becoming lined with books devoted exclusively to the subject. Once you have made your own fresh salsas, those jars of grayish-red stuff "from New York City!!???" will be banished from your pantry for all eternity.

Although it matters little to the taste of the finished product, uniformly diced fruits and vegetables make a more attractive salsa.

1. When cutting tomatoes, chiles, and peppers, trim the ends first and cut out the seeds and pith from the inside. The hearts of the tomatoes can be reserved for soups and stocks. Cut the vegetables into strips and then into dice.

2. When dicing melons and papayas, peel and seed the fruits, then cut them into even wedges. Trim the individual wedges and cut them into even dice. Or, melons, papayas, and mangos may be peeled and cut away from the seeds in even "planks," which may then be evenly diced in the same manner as tomatoes and chiles. The yield will be slightly less, but the dice will be much more uniform. The method also saves a little time.

3. Combine the salsa ingredients in a bowl and mix just until well blended. Taste and adjust the seasoning. Stir salsas gently and briefly to avoid mangling or bruising the ingredients.

what not to do

1. Remember that the joy of salsas lies in their freshness. Their flavor is improved by sitting at room temperature for up to 1 hour, but after that they begin to lose their texture. Avoid making more than you need for one meal.

2. Use fruits and vegetables that are ripe but still firm. Perfectly ripe foods are difficult to dice and will become mushy when the other ingredients are added.

3. Overmixing turns diced fresh vegetables and fruits into mush, so try to get the seasoning as close as possible the first time you taste, season, and stir.

salsa fresca

makes about 1 cup

This is a version of the classic fresh salsa, or pico de gallo, which is a natural to serve with grilled meats and seafoods. The good Mexican beer called for adds a distinct and amazingly refreshing note.

$^1/_4$ **red onion, diced**

4 ripe Roma tomatoes, diced

1 to 2 jalapeño chiles, diced

2 tablespoons coarsely chopped cilantro leaves

1 teaspoon salt

Pinch of sugar

1 tablespoon fresh lime juice

1 teaspoon olive oil

2 tablespoons good Mexican or dark beer (optional)

Put the onion in a sieve and run it under warm water for 3 to 4 seconds to rinse it. Drain the onion well and put it in a bowl with the tomatoes and all the remaining ingredients except the beer. Stir the salsa gently and briefly to blend the herbs and spices. Pour the beer over and stir just to blend. Taste and adjust the seasoning. Cover and allow to stand for 30 minutes before serving at room temperature.

Salsa Fresca (top), Papaya and Black Bean Salsa (center), and Dry Roasted Corn and Sweet Pepper Salsa over grilled chicken breasts dusted with Jimmy the B's Wildcat Barbeque Spice Rub

dry-roasted corn and sweet pepper salsa

makes about 1 ¹/₂ cups

Most recipes for dry-roasted corn salsas call for ingredients that reinforce the almost smoky flavor of the corn, such as mushrooms, marjoram or thyme, and sherry or balsamic vinegar. This recipe heads in the other direction, using the fresh flavors of cilantro and rice vinegar to contrast with the woodsiness of the corn. Serve it with grilled salmon or other fish, or with pork, chicken, or rabbit.

1 cup fresh corn kernels (about 2 large ears), dry-roasted (see page 116)

¹/₄ cup diced red bell pepper

¹/₂ large jalapeño chile, seeded and diced

2 teaspoons coarsely chopped cilantro

2 tablespoons diced red onion

1 tablespoon olive oil

Salt to taste

Ground black pepper to taste

¹/₄ teaspoon plain rice wine vinegar

Juice of ¹/₄ lime, or to taste

Spread the roasted corn kernels out in a shallow pan to cool completely. In a medium bowl, combine the corn and all of the remaining ingredients together and stir until just blended. Taste the salsa and adjust the seasoning. Cover and let salsa sit for 30 minutes before serving.

papaya and black bean salsa

makes about 2 cups

This is a good salsa to serve with swordfish or scallops. The buttery texture of the fruit complements the texture of seafood perfectly. It also goes well with grilled chicken, and tuna carpaccio and tartare. If you would like, substitute mango for the papaya, though you will probably need a bit less lime juice.

1 tablespoon diced red onion

1 large papaya, peeled and diced

¹/₄ cup cooked black beans, rinsed and drain well

1 tablespoon coarsely chopped fresh basil

2 tablespoons diced red bell pepper

¹/₂ teaspoon diced serrano chile

¹/₂ teaspoon salt or to taste

Pinch of freshly ground black pepper

2 teaspoons honey

2 teaspoons fresh lime juice

1 ¹/₂ teaspoons balsamic vinegar

1 tablespoon olive oil

Put the red onion in a sieve and run warm water over it for 2 to 3 seconds to rinse it. Drain the onion well and put it in a medium bowl with all the remaining ingredients. Stir the ingredients until they are just blended. Taste and adjust the seasoning. Let sit for 30 minutes at room temperature, and chill slightly before serving.

escabeches

Although the technique was adopted by southwestern cooks centuries ago, escabeche originated in Arab cultures. The word means to pickle or to souse, and the practice was originally used to prevent spoilage in fish and meats. Vinegars and citrus juices were infused with herbs and spices, then poured over cooked meats to cover them. The Moors brought the technique to Spain, and the Spanish brought it to Mexico and points north and south. Although the methods and some of the recipes have changed little over the ages, escabeches are now enjoyed simply for their tart and original flavors. Modern recipes for meats and fish *en escabeche* are still common, but it is in the preparation of vegetables that the tart, spicy flavors really shine. Because they are simple, hearty, and easy to prepare, escabeches are bound to become some of your favorite salads and side dishes. Since they usually contain no oils or other added fats, these recipes are healthy and low in calories. Once you feel comfortable with the basic preparations, feel free to experiment with your own brine and vegetable combinations.

1. Bring the vinegar and other liquid ingredients to a boil. Lower the heat to a simmer and add the spices. If infusing the brine with fresh herbs such as basil or cilantro, add them to the brine just before straining and serving.

2. Thinly sliced soft vegetables such as onion or pepper rings and tomatillos can be wilted and pickled by simply pouring the hot strained brine over them.

3. Denser vegetables such as carrots and parsnips are usually cooked directly in the strained brine. Because of their high

starch content, potatoes are blanched separately, rinsed, then added to the brine to prevent it from clouding.

4. Stir in any fresh green herbs just before serving, then drain the brine. (Not pictured.) Brines may be refrigerated and used once or twice more.

what not to do

1. **Don't try to get too much mileage out of brines. They are usually good for only 2 batches. If it has been a few days or a week since you have used it, taste a brine before using it again. If the flavors are muddled and it no longer tastes fresh, discard it and start a new one. If the brine feels slick or oily, then it has spoiled. Be sure to bring the brine to a complete boil before each use.**

2. **Avoid blemished, bruised vegetables or ones that are just a bit past their prime. Vegetables that are less than firm will wither and lose their color, and a lightly bruised tomatillo can darken to reddish brown when pickled.**

3. **Be careful when adding salt. Many different brands and types of vinegar contain more salt than others, and most citrus juices seem to bring out a salty quality in escabeches.**

nopalitos escabeche with roasted corn and roma tomatoes

makes about 6 cups

In the late spring, the tender new pads, or noaples, of the prickly pear cactus are harvested. The crisp texture of the cooked flesh is reminiscent of asparagus and okra, and it is wonderful in escabeches and salsas.

4 **medium cactus pads, about 2 pounds**

1 $^1/_4$ **cups rice vinegar**

$^1/_2$ **cup water**

$^1/_2$ **cup sugar**

1 **large jalapeño, split**

1 **sprig cilantro**

$^1/_4$ **teaspoon salt or to taste**

3 **medium ears of corn**

2 **large Roma tomatoes, seeded and diced**

$^1/_4$ **cup coarsely chopped, tightly packed cilantro leaves**

4 **tablespoons chopped scallions**

Bring at least 1 gallon of lightly salted water to a strong simmer over medium-high heat. Wearing heavy gloves, carefully trim away the needles and any dark spots from the cactus with a sharp knife. Cut the pads into strips about 3 inches long and $^1/4$ inch wide. Blanch the cactus for 2 to 3 minutes or until it is brightly colored and al dente. Drain the cactus into a colander and plunge it into ice water. If necessary, the cactus may be blanched and shocked again quickly to remove any remaining slime.

Place the vinegar, water, and sugar into a pot and bring to a boil over medium-high heat. Reduce to a simmer, add the jalapeño, and cook for 1 minute more. Remove the pot from the stove and add the cilantro sprig. Let the brine sit for 1 or 2 minutes or until the flavors have developed but the brine is still hot. Strain the liquid over the cactus and allow it to cool to room temperature. Cover and chill for 4 hours to overnight.

Cut the corn from the cob and dry-roast (see page 116). Spread the kernels out in a shallow pan and allow them to cool to room temperature, then chill (can be done up to 24 hours in advance). When ready to serve, drain the chilled cactus, reserving the brine for future use if desired, and toss with the tomatoes, the chopped cilantro, scallions, and corn. Put back just enough of the brine to moisten the escabeche. Add salt if needed and serve at once.

peach, canela, and star anise escabeche

makes 2 to 3 cups

This sweet-hot escabeche is a good side dish to serve with ham or grilled pork or chicken. The dried fruit tones of guajillo chiles make them the perfect choice to complement the sweetness of fruit and give it some bite. Plums work well in this dish, too, and have the added benefit of not needing to be peeled.

6 peaches, peeled and pitted, or 8 plums, pitted

$^1/2$ cup champagne or white wine vinegar

$^1/4$ cup water

Six 2-inch sticks canela, or 4 sticks cinnamon

2 pods star anise

2 teaspoons finely diced seeded guajillo chile

$^1/2$ cup honey + 1 tablespoon

$^1/2$ cup sugar

$^1/4$ teaspoon salt or to taste

Cut the peaches or plums into wedges about $^1/2$ inch thick. In a small nonreactive saucepan, combine all of the ingredients except for the peaches. Bring to a simmer over moderate heat and cook for 3 to 4 minutes, or until the brine is well infused. Add half of the fruit to the simmering brine and cook for 1 to 2 minutes until the fruit softens slightly. Using a slotted spoon, remove the peach or plum wedge to a bowl and repeat the process with the remaining fruit. Let cool, then cover and refrigerate for at least 3 hours to overnight.

To serve, drain the fruit. If desired, leave the star anise and cinnamon sticks in for an inedible garnish. Reserve the brine for the next batch, if desired.

tomatillo and pepper-ring escabeche with garlic

makes about 6 cups

This is a great side dish to serve with sandwiches in place of slaw or fries. It also goes well with sausages and roasted fowl. As with all escabeches, be sure to serve it well chilled.

1 red bell pepper

1 yellow bell pepper

1 large poblano chile

$^1/_2$ onion, cut into $^1/_4$-inch-thick slices

5 to 6 large tomatillos, soaked in warm water for 30 minutes, husked, and cut into quarters

6 to 8 cloves garlic, halved

FOR THE BRINE

4 cups rice wine vinegar

2 cups water

2 pods star anise

4 sticks canela or 2 sticks cinnamon, cracked

1 $^1/_4$ teaspoons dried thyme

2 teaspoons fennel seed

1 $^1/_4$ teaspoons whole allspice

2 teaspoons coriander seed

4 cloves

6 serranos, halved

1 dried New Mexico red chile, split, stemmed, and seeded

1 $^1/_2$ cups sugar

$^1/_4$ bunch fresh cilantro

Trim the stem ends of the peppers and poblano. Seed and devein while keeping the peppers and poblano intact, and cut them into $^1/_4$-inch-thick rings. Put all the vegetables except the garlic in a large heat-resistant bowl.

Combine all of the brine ingredients except for the cilantro in a large nonreactive saucepan and bring to a simmer over moderate heat. Reduce the brine by one third, about 8 to 12 minutes. Remove from heat, add the cilantro, and let steep.

Strain the brine into another large saucepan and bring it to a boil. Reduce the heat to low, add the garlic and cook for 2 to 4 minutes, or until the garlic is tender but not mushy. Pour the brine over the vegetables and let them cool to room temperature, uncovered. When cool, cover and refrigerate the escabeche for at least 6 hours or overnight. When ready to serve, drain off the brine and reserve it for another use.

Tomatillo and Pepper-Ring Escabeche with Garlic (center), Peach, Canela, and Star Anise Escabeche (in jar), and Nopalitos Escabeche with Dry-Roasted Corn and Roma Tomatoes (bottom)

dry rubs and spice pastes

From the flaming open pits of coastal Africa, to the tandoori ovens of India, to the barbecue shacks of rural Alabama, spice rubs and pastes have been flavoring foods almost since the discovery of fire. Originally employed as a preservative, and probably as camouflage for meats that were past their prime, these simple coatings have endured the tests of the ages. In India, dried chiles are ground with aromatic spices such as cardamom, cinnamon, and cloves. Vibrant turmeric and a range of other spices are blended in to make aromatic masalas, of which curry powder is a relative. In Middle Eastern countries, pistachios, sesame seeds, and almonds are ground with aromatics to yield **zaatars,** which coat fish and chicken wonderfully. And in Texas, they have been slathering ribs, whole pigs, and sides of beef with hedonistic chile molido and cayenne-based rubs since the dawn of the cattle drive. Whether as a prelude to saucing or glazing, or as a simple way to add flavors to meals on the run, dry rubs and spice pastes are an important part of the southwestern culinary palette.

Of course, cooks everywhere are constantly looking for ways to add flavor and texture to foods without adding calories. Spice rubs are a good way to crust lean meats that have been trimmed of all their fat, and they also allow for sautéing without oil. They can be perfect for those frequent occasions when you only have thirty minutes to put dinner on the table but don't want to sacrifice flavor. Rubs and pastes can easily become an indispensable fixture in your pantry, since they enhance and flavor foods without the need for a sauce or much further embellishment. Here is where buying whole spices such as cumin and coriander seed and grinding them yourself pays the highest dividends. The nutty, rich flavors and aromas are worth the small effort required. If you don't have a spice or coffee grinder, you can grind large quantities in a good blender. It is preferable, however, to buy a grinder just for spices and to keep the quantities small and fresh.

1. Measure all ingredients carefully. Toast any dried herbs and spices (see page 117). If using whole spices, transfer them to a spice grinder or blender and grind them until smooth. If you are grinding large amounts of spices in a blender, you can add the other ingredients to the spices and pulse until all the ingredients are well blended. Otherwise, stir all the ingredients together well in a bowl. For pastes, grind and blend all of the dried spices first, then transfer the mixture to a bowl, pour in the liquid, and mix well.

2. Small pieces of food such as chicken breasts and pork chops can be dusted or rubbed up to 1 hour ahead of time. Larger cuts of meat such as leg of lamb and prime rib should be coated from 12 to 24 hours in advance.

what not to do

1. When cooking smaller cuts of meat, chicken, or fish, don't put the rubs or pastes on more than 1 or 2 hours before cooking. Thinner cuts should not be dusted until the last minute. Not only might the spices overwhelm the taste of the meat, but the salts and sugars could coagulate the proteins. Just as gravlax and ceviches are cured by salts and sugars, your food might be "cooked" before it ever gets close to heat.

2. Even though it works beautifully for our Cajun friends, avoid blackening the surfaces of the meats when you sear them. Cajun spice mixes are designed specifically for blackening, and some other spice rubs will coincidentally blacken well without bitterness. As a general rule, however, the age-old rule of the kitchen applies: brown—good, black—bad.

3. Don't try to "eyeball" recipes. Many cooks have ruined rub recipes (and subsequently expensive cuts of meat) by pouring what they presume to be 2 teaspoons of cayenne or chile molido, when in fact it was either half or double that. Get out the measuring spoons!

jimmy the b's wildcat barbecue spice rub

makes about $^1/_4$ cup

Red Sage dining chef James Bondoc uses this rub to give a barbecued flavor to meats, poultry, and scallops. It is a hearty rub with a broad range of uses, and it coats and colors foods nicely as they cook. Red Sage uses another spice rub known as "napalm." Consisting of equal parts ground black pepper, white pepper, chile molido, and kosher salt, it isn't nearly as lethal as it sounds. It's a good all-purpose seasoning for grilled meats.

2 $^1/_2$ pieces dried chipotle chiles

$^3/_4$ teaspoon cumin seed

$^1/_2$ teaspoon coriander seed

2 teaspoons diced sun-dried tomatoes, not packed in oil (optional)

2 $^1/_2$ teaspoons sugar

1 $^1/_2$ teaspoon salt

$^1/_2$ teaspoon dry mustard

$^1/_4$ teaspoon peppercorns

Toast the chipotles, cumin, and coriander as described on pages 24 and 117. If using the dried tomatoes, put them in a spice grinder with the sugar and other spices. Grind the mixture until the spices are well blended and the tomato is ground. If your grinder blades are dull and the tomatoes do not grind finely enough, sift the rub through a coarse-meshed sieve to remove the large pieces. Store in an airtight container for up to 3 weeks.

citrus and cinnamon rub

makes about ¹/₄ cup

Citrus gives a spark to spice mixes, and in this one, the orange, lime, and lemon rinds mix with the hard-bark spices and gentle heat of the caribe to complement light meats and seafood. This rub colors nicely, but avoid excessive heat as it might burn the fruit peels, leaving them bitter. If you don't have a zester, use a vegetable peeler to remove wide strips of peel, then trim away the bitter white pith from them with a sharp paring knife.

Zest from 2 oranges, 2 limes, and 2 lemons

1 tablespoon ground cinnamon

1 tablespoon paprika

1 ³/₄ teaspoons salt

1 tablespoon packed brown sugar

1 teaspoon curry powder

1 teaspoon chile caribe

¹/₄ teaspoon peppercorns

¹/₂ teaspoons ground coriander

Preheat the oven to 225°. Put the citrus zest in a shallow pan and dry them in the oven for 20 to 30 minutes, or until they are leathery but not browned. Let cool completely. Put the cool peels in a spice grinder with the remaining ingredients and grind until the peels are pulverized. Store in an airtight container for up to 3 weeks.

cascabel and wild mushroom paste

makes about 1 cup

This simple recipe provides a rich, deep-flavored paste with precious little effort. Leave out the olive oil, and it becomes a dry rub. When made into a spice paste as directed here, it brings a rich flavor to quail, squab, and venison. As when grinding most chiles, it is important to first lightly toast the cascabels. Although they will be leathery and pliable when warm, they will crisp as they cool, allowing a finer grind.

12 to 14 cascabel chiles, stemmed, seeded, and toasted (see page 24)

2 ounces dried mushrooms, preferably porcinis

2 teaspoons dried thyme

1 ¹/₂ teaspoons salt

¹/₄ cup olive oil

Let the chiles cool completely. If using dried mushrooms, put them in a spice grinder and grind to a powder. Transfer the mushroom powder to a small bowl. Put the cooled chiles and thyme in the spice grinder in batches and grind to a powder. Add to the mushroom powder and stir in the salt and olive oil. Slather the paste over meat or fowl, cover, and refrigerate. Squab and venison should sit overnight, quail for 2 to 3 hours. Store the paste in an airtight container in the refrigerator for up to 4 days.

SPICE RUB VARIATION: To use as a spice rub, don't add the oil. Use on chicken, scallops, and other mild foods. Store in an airtight container for up to 3 weeks. Makes ³/₄ cup.

drying meat for jerky

For centuries, Native Americans preserved surplus venison and buffalo by slicing it into thin strips and hanging it in the air to dry. On cattle drives, early settlers slaughtered injured steers, and meat not consumed right away was thinly sliced and hung over cords to dry in the sun. Cowboys too ravenous to wait for the chuck wagon would gnaw on the leathery shreds while they tended to the herd. In cooler climates, where the drying process could take days, less nomadic folks hung the strips from branches or rafters, safe from voracious dogs and wolves. Burlap or other cloth was draped over the jerky as it dried, and at night the meat was taken indoors to keep nocturnal varmints from enjoying a free buffet.

By comparison, the chores required to make jerky today are practically effortless. The coarse, tenacious texture and potent flavors of dried meat go well with chiles and spices and yield strips that make wonderful, long-lived snacks. They can also be used to add a unique robustness to sauces and can be cut into fine strips and diced to garnish salads, soups, and stuffings. Choose relatively lean cuts of meat that have little sinew, such as top or bottom rounds. For hunters, jerky is a great way to preserve cuts from the legs and flanks that might otherwise end up as hamburger, and it yields a terrific snack for the next adventure into the woods.

1. Trim the exterior of the meat of all visible fat, silverskin, and sinew. Place it in the freezer for 1 to 1 1/2 hours, or until it is firm enough to slice thinly but is not frozen solid. While waiting for the meat to firm up, make the marinade or any spice mixture or rub called for in the recipe. Using either a sharp slicing knife or a mechanical slicer, slice the meat with the grain into long thin slices about 1/16 inch thick. Thinner cuts of meat can be sliced on the bias, to yield wider strips.

2. Depending on the recipe and level of spice desired, either marinate the meat, dredge it in the spice rub, or lay the strips on a wire rack or grill screen and sprinkle the spice over them.

3. Preheat the oven to 400°. Place the oven rack on the middle shelf of the oven and turn off the oven. Prop the door open slightly. It may be necessary to use a small ball of aluminum foil to hold the door open about 1 inch. Let the meat dry for at least 3 to 4 hours or overnight. Because all ovens are built and vented differently, drying times will vary. After 2 to 3 hours, check the oven. If it has cooled completely and the meat is still not dry, turn the oven on again for 5 or 6 minutes to get it hot again, leaving the meat inside. After turning off the oven for the second time, the jerky should be done within 30 minutes to 1 hour. Jerky should be slightly flexible and chewy, not stiff and chalky.

what not to do

1. **Don't slice the meat too thinly or thickly. The ideal thickness is about $1/16$-inch thick. If it's sliced too thin, the spices will overwhelm the flavor of the meat and the jerky will dry too quickly. Slabs of jerky that are too thick might spoil before they dry or may be too difficult to chew. If necessary, place the strips of meat between pieces of plastic wrap and pound them lightly to the desired thinness.**

2. **Until you are comfortable with the process, check the jerky after the first hour. All ovens are different, and the times given above are only guidelines. Your oven could produce jerky in much less time, or considerably more.**

3. **Every butcher in America has been trained to always cut meat across the grain. Making cuts perpendicular to the direction of the connective tissues results in a more tender slice of meat. However, jerkies that are cut in this manner can be too soft and lack that snap-your-head-back quality that makes these morsels so enjoyable. Always slice meats for jerkies *with* the grain.**

smoky barbecued beef jerky

makes 10 to 14 slices

This recipe approximates the aroma and flavor of the smokehouse without requiring you to split any kindling or rub sticks together. Oven-dried jerkies are so easy to make that they could become a standard ingredient in your culinary back of tricks. This one is full of flavor and great for snacking, but it is also wonderful when cut into julienne strips and sprinkled over salads.

$2^1/2$ tablespoons Chipotles en Adobo Purée (page 26)

$1/3$ cup Jay's Quick and Easy Barbecue Sauce (page 121) or a premium brand

1 pound beef top or bottom round, trimmed, chilled, and sliced (see page 45)

2 teaspoons kosher salt or to taste

Freshly ground black pepper to taste

Pour the chipotle purée and barbecue sauce into a small bowl and stir well to blend. Pour this mixture over the meat and stir just enough to coat the meat without mangling it. Let set at room temperature for 30 minutes to 1 hour.

Preheat the oven to 400°. Spread the meat slices out on a wire rack or grill screen. The meat slices should be just lightly coated with the marinade. Sprinkle lightly with the salt and a few twists of pepper from the pepper mill.

Place the oven rack on the middle shelf of the oven and turn off the oven. Prop the door open slightly with a ball of aluminum foil. Let the meat dry for at least 3 to 4 hours or overnight, or until the jerky is slightly flexible and chewy. Store, tightly wrapped, in the refrigerator, for up to 10 days.

Smoky Barbecued Beef Jerky (in pot), Blackberry and Balsamic Venison Jerky (right)

blackberry and balsamic venison jerky

makes 10 to 14 slices

In the crisp, dry autumn air, Native Americans hung strips of venison over forked branches to dry with the corn, squashes, and chiles that were vital for their sustenance during the bitter winter months. The jerky was often mixed in with dried chokeberries or apples and suet to make pemmican, another winter staple. Venison, blackberry, and honey are an inspired combination, and guajillos provide a subtle and complementary heat.

$^1/_2$ **cup fresh blackberries**

2 tablespoons Guajillo Purée or to taste (page 26)

2 tablespoons balsamic vinegar or to taste

2 $^1/_2$ tablespoons honey or to taste

$^3/_4$ **teaspoon fresh-cracked black pepper or to taste**

Kosher salt to taste

1 pound venison, trimmed, chilled, and sliced (see page 45)

Put the blackberries in a blender with the guajillo purée, vinegar, and honey and process until smooth. Taste to adjust the seasoning. Strain the marinade through a medium-meshed sieve and stir in the pepper and salt. Pour the marinade over the meat and stir to just coat it without mangling. Let it sit at room temperature for 30 minutes to 1 hour. Preheat the oven to 400°. Drain the meat and spread the strips out on a wire rack or grill screen. The marinade should coat the meat lightly. Place the oven rack on the middle shelf of the oven and turn off the oven. Prop the door open slightly with a ball of aluminum foil. Let the meat dry for at least 3 to 4 hours or overnight, or until the jerky is flexible and chewy. Store, tightly covered, in the refrigerator for up to 1 week.

grilling

In an increasingly health-conscious age, grilling is frequently the cooking method of choice. Grilling allows fats to drain away from foods instead of cooking them in, and adds a delectable crust and a smoky woodsiness that is a perfect foil for the flavors of the Southwest. Cooking over fire is obviously the oldest and most primal of the cooking methods, and in many minds, the culinary arts took a step backwards when they moved indoors.

For the sake of economy as well as flavor, many restaurants are now grilling over hardwoods such as hickory, pecan, and mesquite, as well as with alder and fruit woods such as apple and cherry. Each wood adds its own unique character (see page 50). For backyard grilling, lump hardwood charcoal is probably the practical fuel of choice. It burns hot and adds a light flavor to grilled foods, while charcoal briquettes, the staple of the backyard cookout, are made of compressed sawdust that has had any nuance of wood flavor burned out of it. Drained soaked wood chips can be sprinkled over the coals to add more flavor to grilled foods. A variety of wood chips are available at most good kitchenware shops and specialty foods stores.

More and more people are turning to the conveniences of the gas or propane grill. Although these methods don't provide the distinct flavor that cooking over wood or charcoal does, soaked wood chips can be used to give a distinctive smoky character. Consult your owner's manual for the most effective way to do this.

Smaller, more tender cuts of meat such as chops and steaks are the best candidates for grilling, as they will crust beautifully and their relatively short cooking times will allow them to retain moisture. Firm fish such as salmon, mahimahi, and swordfish, as well as shrimp, scallops, and lobster, are perfect candidates for the grill, while flaky fish such as sole and flounder should be avoided. Thicker cuts of meat such as whole tenderloins and roasts can be covered and cooked over moderate heat. They may also be seared on the grill to flavor them, then finished in the oven.

1. When building a fire for grilling, make sure that the coals are spread more broadly than the foods to be grilled. There should be a cooler perimeter around the fire to move meats to in case of flare-ups or to allow thicker cuts of meats to cook slowly after being seared. Make sure that the grill rack is clean and hot before placing the meat on it. To prevent sticking, nonmarinated meats should be brushed very lightly with vegetable oil or sprayed with cooking spray.

2. Turn food as often as necessary to prevent burning and to allow even cooking. To make cross-hatch patterns on food, place it on the grill rack and allow it to sear. Turn the food 90 degrees (a one-quarter turn) and continue to

grill until the desired design is achieved. Repeat the process on the other side. If the food is not yet cooked, you will have to decide whether to spoil the precious design or transfer it to the oven to finish cooking.

what not to do

1. **Don't let the flames contact food directly. This will coat food with a black residue that is extremely bitter and is to be avoided at all costs. If it occurs, wipe the residue away with a damp cloth.**

2. **Oil-based marinades should be drained well and the surfaces of meat lightly blotted to prevent excessive flare-ups. Marinades that contain sugar, honey, or molasses burn easily; meat marinated in these must be turned often and can be finished in the oven if necessary.**

3. **Avoid using charcoal lighter fluid. It is bad for the environment and can impart a gassy, chemical taste to food. Charcoal chimneys that use newspaper are effective and easy to use, and can be purchased for around $15.**

tips for grilling

hardwoods

Each type of wood adds its own unique character to food as it is grilled or smoked, and many varieties are available in chip form to add flavor and character to your next cookout. **Hickory** smoke has a distinctive robust flavor. **Pecan**, a close relative of hickory, offers a more subtle but rich and velvety smoke, and is the wood of choice for grilling and smoking in the Southwest. **Mesquite** emits a tangy smoke that is great for grilling chicken and fish. **Apple** and **cherry** offer a mild fruity aroma that is sweeter than other woods; these are great for flavoring fish, chicken, and pork. **Alder** is one of the most commonly used woods in the Pacific Northwest. Its mild and delicate flavors complement grilled and hot-smoked salmon and other fish.

marinades, spice rubs, and glazes

Fine, satisfying meals can be made by simply marinating or spice-rubbing then grilling meat, chicken, and seafood. For more complex dishes, try mixing complementary-flavored marinades and spice rubs with the sauces, salsas, and moles included in this book. For example, swordfish or chicken marinated in Scallion and Cilantro Marinade (page 119) will be complemented by Papaya and Black Bean Salsa (page 36) or Salsa Fresca (page 34). Pork or quail marinated in Canela Brine (page 121) will be well finished by Tamarind-Orange Glaze (page 60) or Cider and Ginger Adobo Glaze (page 59). By using the different recipes as building blocks, many different and satisfying dishes can be created.

testing for doneness

Restaurant chefs judge the doneness of meats and fish by feel, sensing by the resistance of the flesh when the desired level of doneness is achieved. Rare steaks will feel soft and spongy to the touch. Meats cooked to medium rare to medium will feel firm but springy, while medium well to well done steaks will be quite firm. Sirloins and other hearty cuts are tricky in that they will feel firm while they are cooking, but will soften as the meat rests. In *Big Flavors of the Hot Sun*, Chris Schlesinger recommends the "nick, peek, and cheat" method, whereby you remove meat items from the grill, allow them to rest for a moment or two, and cut a small incision into the thickest part and take a look. Fish, being more flexible, can often be "bent" gently to reveal its interior doneness.

grilled onion

Several recipes in this book call for grilled onions. When they are cut into thick rings and cooked over a fire with aromatic wood chips, they take on a delightful smoky quality that imparts to other foods on contact. An added benefit is that grilling onions seems to develop their natural sugar while retaining a crispness that is perfect for salsas and stuffings. Grilling without wood chips doesn't provide the taste but still yields crisp and sweet onions.

To grill onions, prepare a fire in a charcoal or gas grill. If desired, soak $^1/_2$ cup of wood chips in water to cover for 30 minutes. Drain the chips. For a gas grill, put the chips in the smoker, or in an aluminum pie pan with holes punched in the bottom and placed directly on the lava rocks. For a charcoal grill, sprinkle the chips over the coals. Peel and cut the amount of onion desired into $^1/_4$- to $^1/_2$-inch slices. Coat them lightly with olive oil and season them with salt and coarsely ground black pepper to taste. Spread the slices on the grill over hot coals and let them cook for 1 to 2 minutes, then turn and cook on the second side for another minute, or until browned and flexible but still firm. Transfer the slices to a shallow pan to cool.

If grilled onions aren't practical, peel and cut the amount of onions desired into $^1/_4$- to $^1/_2$-inch slices. Place them on a broiler pan or cookie sheet, brush them lightly with olive oil, and grind black pepper over to taste. Place the pan under the broiler and cook onions for 2 to 3 minutes or until they are a deep caramel color. Do not turn them.

herb marinade for grilled vegetables

These days, some of the tastiest things to come off the grill are vegetables. An open fire is a great way to flavor firm vegetables like fennel, pepper, and squash and to give them an appealingly rustic color. Grilling is also one of the most nutritious ways to cook most vegetables, since you are cooking flavor in instead of boiling it out, and any oils or marinades are drained away instead of being cooked in, as they are when sautéed. The following recipe is an all-purpose one, so feel free to create your own flavors using different herbs. If you are grilling vegetables to be used in fillings or salsas using other herbs and strong flavors, simply coat the vegetables lightly with oil, salt, and pepper and eliminate the other seasonings. When recipes call for diced grilled squash, cut the squash lengthwise as discussed below and prepare extra. Then you can trim away the soft seed-pod strip from the center and use a higher proportion of the colorful flesh for dicing.

$^1/_2$ **cup olive oil**

1 large clove garlic, minced

$^1/_3$ **cup tightly packed basil, tarragon, or thyme leaves**

1 serrano chile, minced

$^1/_2$ **tablespoon salt**

$^1/_4$ **tablespoon ground black pepper**

Juice of 1 lime, or to taste

About 2 pounds vegetables, such as portobello mushrooms, fennel, bell peppers, summer squash, zucchini, and so on

In a large bowl, combine all the ingredients except the vegetables. Then toss all the vegetables except the portobellos in this marinade and let them sit at room temperature for 30 minutes to 1 hour.

Portobellos and other mushrooms work best if they are brushed with the marinade, allowed to sit for 1 hour or so, then grilled whole. Cook them for 2 to 3 minutes on each side, or until they are soft throughout. Let cool and cut them into the desired shape.

If you are grilling zucchini and squash to be cut into dice for salsas, stuffings, or garnishes, slice them lengthwise into $^1/_4$- to $^1/_3$-inch slices. If serving them as a vegetable, cut them into slices on an extreme diagonal.

Soak wooden skewers in water for 30 minutes to prevent them from burning. Thread round vegetables and crosswise slices on two parallel skewers to keep them from spinning as they are turned. Peppers and fennel can be cut into wedges. If grilling fennel, trim away the core, but leave enough of it to hold the wedges together as they cook.

Place the marinated vegetables over medium-hot coals and cook for 1 to 3 minutes per side, or until they color and soften. Thicker or denser vegetables can be moved to the cooler perimeter of the fire and allowed to continue cooking. Vegetables may be marked and colored on the grill and finished later in the oven if desired.

range-top smoking

The Native Americans discovered the preservative powers of smoke many centuries ago. To prepare a bountiful catch of fish for winter storage, platforms were built over smoldering fires and cleaned salmon or trout were laid out to absorb the redolent vapors as they dried. The smoke killed most of the bacteria by robbing them of oxygen, while the heat from the fire dried the fish. Fish (and later, meats) that were prepared in this manner could be stored for several months, and they kept many a tribesperson from starving during the leanest of times.

Better means of storage and transport have largely eliminated the need to preserve foods with smoke. Today, smoking is most often done simply for the taste of it. For example, lusciously sweet scallops and shrimp take on a delightful, woodsy taste when hot-smoked, and vegetable-based soups and sauces take on a rich flavor and can help make stockless sauces hearty enough to complement meats and fishes. As opposed to barbecuing, which is a long, slow process that crusts and cooks meat as it smokes, hot-smoking quickly flavors smaller cuts of meats, seafood, and vegetables that are then cooked by other means. Smoked shrimp, chicken, or other meats quickly impart a delightful smoky taste when sautéed with vegetables or added to pastas.

Cold-smoking, which is most often done to flavor and preserve large cuts of meat, slabs of bacon, and whole sides of fish such as salmon, doesn't actually cook food. The proteins of meats and fish are firmed by curing salts and brines, much like gravlax and ceviches. Cold-smoking requires specialized equipment and much trial and error to perfect, and so is not illustrated here.

On page 50, various types of wood and the ways they are commonly paired with foods are briefly discussed. The same guidelines apply to hot-smoking, but feel free to use different woods to suit your personal preference. A wide variety of wood chips are now readily available in many food and kitchen gadget stores, but if you can't locate them in your area, mail-order sources are included in the back of the book.

Restaurant kitchens are designed with excellent exhaust systems that draw away smoke and keep the surrounding air clear. Household ranges are not designed to vent the large volume of smoke this procedure generates, and certain precautions must be taken. The method illustrated below will allow you to smoke on your range, as long as you follow a few simple precautions.

1. Begin with 2 disposable pans at least 10 inches square. One pan should be at least 2 $1/2$ to 4 inches deep, the other 1 $1/2$ to 2 inches deep. Mound 2 tablespoons of fine wood chips in the center of the deep pan. Pour 1 teaspoon of water over the fine chips; if you are using large wood chunks, leave them dry. (Soaking the wood chips completely would require a longer smoking time, which would actually cook the foods.) Using a paring knife or large skewer, perforate the shallow pan at 1- to 1 $1/2$-inch intervals.

2. Taking care not to crowd them, arrange the marinated meats or vegetables in the shallower pan and set it over the pan with the wood chips. Cover both pans tightly with aluminum foil or 2 to 3 layers of plastic wrap, and place them on the range over medium-low heat. (If using an electric range, preheat the element.)

3. Let the pans sit over the heat for $1^{1}/_{2}$ to 2 minutes if using fine chips, 2 to 3 minutes if using larger chunks. Turn off the heat and let the pan sit undisturbed for 2 to 3 minutes.

(If using an electric range, take the pan off the element.) Take the pan outside, close the door behind you, and remove the foil or plastic. If the food smells too smoky or acrid, give it a quick rinse under cold water. Food smoked in this manner is usually better the second day, after the flavors of the food, marinade, and smoke have had a chance to meld.

what not to do

1. **When range-top smoking, *don't* unwrap the pan in the kitchen. The smoke will permeate the entire house and could alienate the affections of everyone in the domicile.**

2. **Due to variations in wood types, pan sizes, and stove tops, hot-smoking is an inexact science and should be treated as such. Prepare extra food the first time you try this, so that you can taste and experiment and try again to achieve an excellent result.**

3. **Almost all food that is hot-smoked should be marinated first. Even the milder woods can deliver a strong taste of smoke during the short but intense hot-smoking times. Marinades and brines with honey, brown sugar, or molasses will help to counter the slightly bitter flavor of smoke. Lime, Brown Sugar, and Hazelnut Marinade (page 51) was developed just for this purpose. In the marinade section that begins on page 118, you will find other recipes that work well with smoked foods.**

4. **If you are using a gas range, there is a small chance that the heat might conduct through the pans and melt the plastic wrap, releasing the smoke. Although using foil won't allow you the excitement of watching the smoke fill the pan, it might be safer.**

smoked sweet red pepper sauce

makes about 1 1/2 cups

This easy, stockless sauce goes well with seafood, pork, and chicken. The optional butter gives it a richness that is worth the few calories that it adds. The key to success here is to not cook the sauce any longer than is necessary to allow the flavors to meld.

2 1/2 tablespoons wood chips

4 red bell peppers, fire-roasted, peeled, and seeded (see pages 18–19)

2 teaspoons olive oil

1 onion, diced

4 large cloves garlic

2 1/2 tablespoons minced peeled fresh ginger

1/4 to 1/2 habanero chile, seeded and diced

1 1/2 cups water

1 1/2 teaspoons salt

1 tablespoon coarsely chopped fresh basil

3 tablespoons honey

Juice of 1 lime

1 1/2 teaspoons cold butter (optional)

Using the wood chips, smoke the red peppers (see pages 54–55). In a large sauté pan or skillet over medium heat, heat the oil and sauté the onion and garlic, stirring occasionally, for 4 to 6 minutes, or until browned and soft. Add the ginger, habanero, and smoked peppers and sauté for 1 minute. Add the water and bring to a boil. Reduce the heat to a simmer and cook for 2 to 3 minutes. Add the salt and transfer the mixture to a blender. Add the basil and purée until smooth.

Return the mixture to the pan, bring to a low simmer, and add the honey and lime juice. For a richer sauce, whisk in the cold butter. Taste and adjust the seasoning, strain the sauce, and keep it warm over hot water until ready to serve.

lime, brown sugar, and hazelnut oil marinade

makes about 1 cup

These three flavors meld perfectly to offset and complement the rich flavor that hot-smoking provides. Scallops, shrimp, or chicken breasts that are marinated and hot-smoked in this manner bring a luscious quality to pastas or stir-fries, and they are great when simply finished on the grill or on the stove.

1/2 cup hazelnut oil

1/4 cup fresh lime juice

2 1/2 tablespoons packed brown sugar

1 3/4 teaspoons minced serrano chile

1 tablespoon chopped fresh rosemary

1 teaspoon salt

1/2 teaspoon ground black pepper

Put all the ingredients in a blender and purée until smooth. Use this mixture to marinate shrimp, scallops, swordfish steaks, and chicken breasts for 1 hour at room temperature before smoking (see pages 54–55). Pork chops or medallions should be marinated in the refrigerator for 2 to 3 hours.

glazing meats and poultry

glaze can be as simple as a hearty barbecue sauce or as complex and multilayered as the most sophisticated of sauces. In both modern and classical kitchens, stocks are often cooked slowly to reduce them to an almost syrupy consistency, concentrating the flavors. These glazes are then added to soups and sauces to fortify and enhance the flavor of the meat from which they were derived. Glazes can also be finished with butter or herbs and brushed onto the surfaces of meat and fowl to flavor them and to provide an elegant and finished look. Since flamboyant chiles and assertive flavors can impose their will on more subtle meats such as chicken and pork, glazes brushed on their surfaces during the last moments of cooking are a great way to reinforce the flavor of the meat. In addition to adding flavor, a good glaze will make roasted or grilled meats glisten. The spicy tones of chiles can be counterpointed and mellowed with a few drops of molasses, honey, or reduced fruit juices, bringing harmony and balance to finished dishes with only a modicum of effort.

A glaze can also be created by simply cooking a portion of the sauce until it is reduced to the proper thickness. Of course, the character of the sauce will change as the volume diminishes, and some corrections may be necessary. Sauces that become too hot as they reduce can be mellowed with a complementary sweetener, and flavors that might have dulled from overreduction can be revitalized with the addition of a few drops of lime or lemon juice. As with any procedure or technique, once you have mastered the few basic guidelines, feel free to play fast and loose with the rules.

1. In a wide pan, sauté garlic, onion, or other vegetables as instructed in the recipe. Add the sauce or stock and other ingredients, bring them to a low simmer, and cook over low heat to reduce the volume. If reducing fairly large amounts of sauce, it may be necessary to strain the glaze into a clean pot once or twice, as solids will collect on the sides of the pot, resulting in a potentially bitter residue.

2. Continue reducing the glaze until it is thick enough to coat a spoon. You may wish to brush some onto the surface of the meat as a test. If the fat in the meat repels the glaze, continue reducing. Two cups of most light stock-based sauces will yield about $1/4$ to $1/2$ cup of glaze, or about enough to coat 1 whole chicken or 6 chops.

3. As with barbecue sauces, glazes can burn fairly quickly when exposed to the flames of the grill or the high heat of roasting. For that reason, and to preserve the gloss and sheen that add so much to the presentation, apply glazes during the last moments of cooking.

what not to do

1. **Do not overreduce the glaze. The flavors will become muddled and cloying, and a too-thick glaze will be impossible to apply evenly. If necessary, adjust the consistency with more stock or a few drops of water. If the sauce is based on a weak stock, it may become bitter or "muddy" before it is thick enough to glaze. Taste the glaze as it reduces and, if necessary, add a drop of cornstarch or whisk in 1 or 2 teaspoons of cold butter to thicken it while the flavors are still fresh.**

2. **Reduce the glaze slowly. Boiling rapidly will cause precious flavor to evaporate along with the steam, and will also cause excessive solids to form around the edges of the pan.**

cider and ginger adobo glaze

makes ³/4 cup glaze (or 2 cups sauce)

Unfiltered apple cider, in addition to having a truer apple flavor, has starches and solids that thicken glazes as they reduce. Filtered cider or apple juice are poor substitutes, as they will become too sweet and syrupy when reduced to the levels required here. This glaze is excellent on chicken or pork, and also works well on grilled swordfish or scallops. This recipe would make a fine sauce by simply removing it from the heat a little earlier. For a more complex blend of flavors, try pairing this glaze with meats and fish that have first been dusted with Citrus and Cinnamon Rub (page 44).

2 teaspoons butter, plus additional 2 teaspoons butter for finishing (optional)

¹/2 onion, diced

4 cups unfiltered apple cider

1 ¹/2 cups chicken stock (page 122)

¹/4 cup plain rice vinegar

3 tablespoons molasses

4 teaspoons cascabel purée (page 26)

Six 2-inch sticks canela, or 3 sticks cinnamon

3 tablespoons diced peeled fresh ginger

1 sprig fresh thyme

¹/2 teaspoon salt or to taste

Fresh lime to taste

In a medium, heavy saucepan, melt 2 teaspoons of the butter over medium heat and sauté the onion until it is browned, about 4 minutes. Add the cider and all the other remaining ingredients except the 2 teaspoons optional butter and lime juice. Bring to a boil, lower the heat to a low simmer, and cook to reduce the liquid by half or until a full, round flavor is developed. Strain the mixture into a smaller saucepan and continue to simmer until it has reduced to 2 cups. If desired, remove half of the liquid and reserve it for use as a sauce.

Cook the remaining liquid to reduce it to the consistency of a glaze. Whisk in the butter during the last few minutes of cooking, if desired. Freshen the flavor with a few drops of lime juice. Brush the glaze over roasted or grilled chicken, quail, or pork during the last few minutes of cooking. For a more intense offering, drizzle the remaining glaze around the meats after plating.

tamarind-orange glaze

makes about ³/4 cup

This full-flavored glaze is wonderful on grilled chicken, pork, or shellfish, and you couldn't ask for an easier recipe unless you were making a glass of water! When you're feeling ambitious, try this on food that has been marinated in Canela Brine (page 121) or dusted with Jimmy the B's Wildcat Barbecue Spice Rub (page 43).

¹/2 cup (5 ounces) packed tamarind paste, with pits and fibers

3 cups fresh orange juice

1 to 2 tablespoons Chipotles en Adobo Purée (page 43)

2 tablespoons packed brown sugar or to taste

1 teaspoon cold butter (optional)

Salt to taste

Put all the ingredients except for the butter and salt in a medium, heavy saucepan and bring to a boil. Reduce the heat to a simmer and cook slowly for 20 to 30 minutes, or until a saucelike consistency is achieved. Strain the glaze into a smaller pan. Taste and adjust the seasoning with brown sugar, chipotle, and salt, if necessary. Cook to reduce to a glaze and, if desired, whisk in the butter just before using. Brush the glaze onto grilled, smoked, or sautéed meats during the last few minutes of cooking.

cowboy coffee and plum barbecue glaze

makes 1¹/2 to 2 cups

This simple and flavorful glaze can be brushed on grilled or sautéed game or hearty steaks such as sirloins. It also makes a nice barbecue glaze for slow-cooked pork ribs.

2 teaspoons butter, plus additional 2 teaspoons butter for finishing (optional)

¹/2 yellow onion, diced

6 ripe plums, pitted and cut into wedges

4 pieces stemmed, seeded, and toasted ancho chile (see page 24)

1¹/2 cups strong brewed coffee

¹/2 cup Jay's Quick and Easy Barbecue Sauce (page 121) or a premium brand

¹/4 cup molasses or to taste

2 teaspoons red wine vinegar

Lime juice to taste

Salt to taste

In a heavy, medium-sized saucepan, melt 2 teaspoons of butter over medium-high heat and sauté the onion until golden brown, about 4 minutes. Add the plums and sauté for 2 to 3 minutes, or until soft. Add the chile, coffee, barbecue sauce, molasses, vinegar, and lime juice. Bring to a simmer and cook until the sauce is reduced by about one third and is full of flavor.

Put the mixture in a blender and purée until smooth. Strain the glaze into a small saucepan and continue reducing if necessary. Taste and adjust the seasonings, adding salt as necessary. If desired, whisk in the optional 2 teaspoons of butter just before brushing the glaze over meat during the last few moments of cooking.

rellenos

Chiles are the perfect vessels for a wide variety of stuffings and fillings. The word *rellenar* means "to stuff," and in Mexico, it is the poblano chile that is traditionally filled with cheese or chorizo and potatoes (or an endless variety of other fillings), then battered and fried. Anchos, guajillos, and other dried chiles have long been rehydrated and stuffed also, but as fresh poblanos, Anaheims, and New Mexico chiles are now available practically year-round, this practice is employed less. Today, chiles rellenos are just as often served without the fried coating, allowing the meaty and buttery nuances of fresh chiles to come through. Stuffed chiles can also be served with their cut sides up to reveal the colors and aromas of their fillings. Cold stuffings such as a fresh seafood salad complement chiles to be served as appetizers or lunch entrées.

Traditional batter coatings can soak up a lot of oil; also, since homemade chiles rellenos must usually be fried in batches and either kept warm or reheated, it is usually preferable to bread them in either cornmeal or Panko (Japanese bread crumbs). They can be kept warm better than battered ones, and the contrast of the crunchy coating against the lush and velvety texture of the chiles is marvelous.

1. Roast and peel the chiles (see pages 18–20). Make an incision down the side of the chile from just under the stem to within 1/2 inch of the tip. Carefully scoop out the seeds and cut out the ribs with a sharp knife. You may want to prepare a few more chiles than the recipe calls for in case one or more are split beyond repair. Minimal tears in the chiles can be fixed by "stitching" them with toothpicks or skewers after they have been stuffed. Make the stuffing according to the chosen recipe and refrigerate it until chilled.

2. Stuff the chiles. If they are to be fried, leave room to fold the seams of the chile over to seal it. If necessary, skewer the scam or any tears in the chile to seal it well, and set it seam-side down. If the chile will not be fried, or if it will be served chilled, you may stuff it as full as you like.

3. Let chiles rellenos set at room temperature for 5 to 10 minutes and coat them just before frying. To coat the chiles,

lightly dredge them in flour, then dip them in eggs that have been beaten with a little milk. Allow the excess egg wash to run off of the chiles, then roll them in yellow or blue cornmeal or Panko (Japanese bread crumbs).

4. To fry the chiles rellenos, heat 5 inches of vegetable oil in a heavy pot or deep-fryer to 350° or until sizzling hot but

not smoking. If cooking the chiles in batches, preheat the oven to 250°. Place one or more rellenos in the oil carefully with a slotted spoon or with your fingers. To ensure even cooking, do not crowd the pot: allow 1 inch of space between each of the chiles. Fry

them for 2 to 3 minutes, or until they are crisp and golden brown. It should not be necessary to turn them. Using a

slotted spoon, remove the chiles from the hot oil and drain on paper towels. Place on a wire rack or grill screen set on a baking sheet in the warm oven. Repeat the process to cook the remaining rellenos. If the chiles have been stuffed with a particularly dense filling such as carnitas, it may be necessary to bake them in a 325° oven for 1 to 2 minutes to warm them through. Serve the rellenos as soon after frying them as possible.

5. To heat uncoated chiles, you may either warm the chiles and filling separately and stuff them right before serving, or stuff them ahead and rewarm them when ready to serve. The first method will provide a more attractive relleno, while the second will be more convenient at service time. To reheat rellenos, preheat the oven to 300°. Place the chiles rellenos in a shallow ovenproof dish and add about $1/2$ inch of water to the dish. Cover the dish with aluminum foil and bake the rellenos for 12 to 15 minutes, or until they are warmed through. Alternatively, place the rellenos on a plate with 2 tablespoons water, cover with plastic wrap, and place in the microwave on medium for 1 to 2 minutes, or until hot.

what not to do

1. **If you are stuffing chiles to fry later, don't use a warm filling. Allow the stuffing to cool completely to prevent any possibility of spoilage.**

2. **Don't over-bread the chiles: drain the excess egg wash from them before rolling them briefly in meal or bread crumbs. If the breading becomes lumpy or clots on the surface of the chile, sift it or discard it and start fresh.**

grilled picadillo rellenos

*makes 4 large rellenos;
serves 4 for appetizer or light entrée*

In Mexican cooking, picadillo *generally refers to a ground or minced pork filling that is mixed with raisins and almonds. This is the classic filling for the chiles rellenos served in restaurants and roadside stands in Oaxaca and other Mexican cities. In this easier version, grilled chicken and onions are substituted for slow-cooked pork. This relleno is coated and fried, but it is also good simply warmed (see Variation). This recipe omits the cheese that is called for in many relleno recipes, but for a richer result, you may add $1/4$ cup grated smoked mozzarella or Monterey jack cheese to the filling.*

FOR THE FILLING

1 whole skinless, boneless chicken breast
   (about 8 ounces)

$1 1/2$ teaspoons salt

1 large Roma tomato, fire-roasted (see pages 18–19)
   and diced

$1/4$ cup diced grilled onion, about $1/2$ small onion
   (see page 51)

2 cloves garlic, dry-roasted and coarsely chopped
   (see page 116)

3 tablespoons raisins, soaked in $1/2$ cup water for
   5 minutes

3 tablespoons sliced almonds, toasted (see page 117)

$3/4$ teaspoon ground cinnamon

$3/4$ teaspoon ground cumin

Pinch of ground coriander

Pinch of ground cloves

$1/4$ cup Jay's Quick and Easy Barbecue Sauce (page 121)
   or a premium brand

2 tablespoons Ancho Chile Purée (see page 26)

1 teaspoon Chiles de Árbol Puree (page 26) or
   a few drops of Tabasco sauce (optional)

3 tablespoons sliced almonds, toasted (see page 117)

4 poblano or fresh New Mexico green chiles, fire-roasted,
   peeled, and prepared for rellenos (see page 61–62)

FOR THE COATING

2 eggs

$1/4$ cup milk

$3/4$ cup all-purpose flour

$1 1/2$ teaspoons salt

$3/4$ cup cornmeal or Panko (Japanese bread crumbs)

$1 1/2$ cups Chile Seco Salsa (page 23)

$3/4$ cup Jay's Quick and Easy Barbecue sauce (page 121)
   or a premium brand

Peanut or corn oil for frying

For the filling, season the chicken with the salt. Grill or broil the chicken for 2 to 3 minutes per side, or until cooked through but not dry. Let the chicken cool to the touch and cut into $1/2$-inch dice. Put the chicken in a bowl with all of the remaining filling ingredients and stir to blend.

Taste and adjust the seasoning. If you are making the filling ahead, don't add the almonds until just before you stuff the chiles.

Preheat the oven to 250°. Stuff the chiles with the filling and place them seam-side down. If stuffing them in advance, cover and refrigerate for up to 24 hours. Let the chiles set at room temperature for 5 to 10 minutes before coating and frying.

For the coating, beat the eggs and milk together in a shallow bowl. Mix the salt and cornmeal together in a shallow bowl. Dredge the chiles in the flour, then in the egg mixture. Drain the excess egg mixture from the chiles, then roll them in the cornmeal until they are lightly coated.

In a medium saucepan, stir the chile salsa and barbecue sauce together and warm them over low heat. Set aside and keep warm.

In a large, heavy pot or deep-fryer, heat 5 inches of the oil to 350°, or until sizzling hot but not smoking. Using a slotted spatula, add 2 stuffed chiles to the oil and cook for 1 to 2 minutes, or until golden brown. Transfer the chiles to a wire rack or grill screen set on a baking pan and place it in the warm oven. Repeat the process to cook the remaining chiles. Serve at once, with the warm sauce drizzled around the rellenos.

VARIATION: To heat and serve the chiles without coating and frying them, substitute slivered almonds for the sliced almonds in the filling. Heat the chiles as described on page 62.

goat cheese and grilled vegetable rellenos

makes 6 rellenos

Having spent several pages explaining how you don't necessarily have to fry rellenos, please allow me one contradiction. The hearty filling of this relleno has a great, strong flavor, but its soft texture cries out for the crunch that cornmeal or Japanese bread crumbs and a short trip to the fryer will provide. Tips for grilling vegetables can be found on page 52.

FOR THE FILLING

2 large portobello mushrooms, stemmed, grilled, and diced

2 zucchini, grilled and diced

1 cup fresh corn kernels (about 1 ear), dry-roasted (see page 116)

2 small chiles, roasted, peeled, and diced (see pages 18–19)

³/₄ cup sliced scallions, green part only (about ¹/₂ bunch)

8 large cloves garlic, dry-roasted and coarsely chopped (see page 116)

4 teaspoons minced fresh marjoram

2 teaspoons ground cumin, toasted (see page 117)

1 ¹/₂ teaspoons ground coriander, toasted (see page 117)

1 teaspoon minced Chipotles en Adobo (page 25)

1 teaspoon adobo sauce from Chipotles en Adobo

Freshly ground black pepper to taste

¹/₂ cup (4 ounces) crumbled fresh goat cheese

6 poblano or fresh New Mexico green chiles, roasted, peeled, and prepared for rellenos (see pages 61–62)

FOR THE COATING

2 eggs

¹/₄ cup milk

1 ¹/₂ teaspoons salt

³/₄ cup cornmeal or Panko (Japanese bread crumbs)

³/₄ cup all-purpose flour

Corn or peanut oil for frying

2 cups Fire-Roasted Tomato and Scotch Bonnet Salsa (page 21), slightly warmed

For the filling, put all the ingredients for the filling except the goat cheese in a medium bowl and stir to blend. Fold in the goat cheese. Taste and adjust the seasoning and stir just to blend. Stuff the chiles loosely and place them seam-side down. If making in advance, cover and refrigerate the chiles for up to 24 hours.

Preheat the oven to 250°. If the rellenos have been refrigerated, let them set at room temperature for 5-10 minutes.

For the coating, beat the eggs and milk together in a shallow bowl. Mix the salt and cornmeal together in a shallow bowl. Dredge the chiles in the flour, then in the egg mixture. Drain the excess egg mixture from the chiles, then roll them in the cornmeal or Panko until they are lightly coated.

In a large heavy pot or deep-fryer, heat 5 to 6 inches of the oil to 350°, or until sizzling but not smoking. Using a

Chilled Rellenos Stuffed with Spicy Shrimp and Scallops (upper right), Goat Cheese and Grilled Vegetable Rellenos (bottom center)

slotted spatula, add 2 to 3 chiles to the oil and fry them 3 to 5 minutes, or until golden brown and warmed through, turning as needed. Using a slotted spatula, transfer the chiles to paper towels to drain. Place the chiles on a wire or grill screen set on a baking sheet and put the pan in the warm oven. Repeat the process to fry the remaining chiles. Serve at once, with the salsa either on the side or drizzled around the rellenos.

chilled rellenos stuffed with spicy shrimp and scallops

makes 4 rellenos

This is a relleno for the new millennium if ever there was one. In contrast to the satisfying and luscious Goat Cheese and Grilled Vegetable Rellenos (page 64), these are lean and practically exploding with fat-free flavor (not counting a little olive oil, which may easily be omitted). The main recipe calls for the seafood to be sliced thin and marinated ceviche style. The Variation has a firmer-textured filling, with shrimp and scallops that are marinated whole for a briefer period, then sautéed.

6 large sea scallops (about 1 pound)

6 large shrimp (about 1 pound), peeled and deveined

1 1/4 cups Orange-Chipotle Marinade (page 119)

Juice of 2 limes

2 tablespoons Grilled Onion (page 51)

2 tablespoons fresh corn kernels, dry-roasted (see page 116)

2 tablespoons finely diced celery

1/4 cup finely diced red bell pepper

2 tablespoons cooked black beans, rinsed

2 tablespoons chopped basil

4 1/2 teaspoons olive oil

4 poblano chiles, roasted, peeled, and prepared for rellenos (see page 61–62)

Cut the scallops into thin crosswise slices. Split the shrimp lengthwise and cut each half into 1/2-inch pieces. Put the shellfish in a nonreactive pan. Combine the marinade and lime juice and stir to blend well. Pour the marinade over the shellfish, cover, and refrigerate for 24 hours. Drain the seafood well and reserve the marinade.

Pour the marinade into a medium saucepan and bring it to a boil. Reduce the heat to a simmer and cook to reduce the liquid to a saucelike consistency, about 3/4 cup, occasionally skimming the foam that rises to the top. Strain the marinade, cover, and refrigerate.

Put the shellfish and all the remaining ingredients except for the marinade reduction, olive oil, and peeled chiles in a medium bowl and stir well to blend. Pour 2 teaspoons of olive oil and half of the chilled marinade over the shellfish and stir to coat it lightly. Taste and adjust the seasoning. Spoon the filling into the chiles until they are quite full. Place the rellenos on chilled serving plates, seam-side up. Pour the marinade reduction around the chiles and drizzle the 2 1/2 teaspoons of the remaining olive oil over it. Serve at once.

VARIATION: Leave the shrimp and scallops whole. Follow the above recipe, marinating them for only 2 hours. Drain the shellfish well, reserving the marinade. In a large nonstick sauté pan or skillet over medium heat, heat 1/4 teaspoon of the olive oil and sauté the shellfish for 1 to 2 minutes. Let cool and cut the shellfish into 1/2-inch dice.

empanadas

mpanadas take their name from *empanar*, Spanish for "to bake in a pastry," and these spicy and luscious turnovers inspire an endless array of filling possibilities. From cooked sausage to carnitas to simple concoctions made with cheese, jalapeños, and fresh herbs, virtually anything you like can be used as a filling for empanadas. The dough possibilities are almost as broad as the fillings themselves. In this section you will find a recipe that uses barbecue spices for a distinct flavor, one that uses yellow or blue cornmeal for a nutty crunch, and one that uses ripe bananas to replace a large measure of the butter that gives these doughs their tenderness.

In Mexico and South America, it is common to see *empanadas gallegas*, which are massive empanadas large enough to serve an entire family. On this side of the border, it is more common to encounter *empanaditas*, or bite-sized morsels served 3 to 4 to a portion as an appetizer or passed as an hors d'oeuvre with a dipping sauce. In this small incarnation, when the proportion of dough to filling is relatively high, it is especially important to make sure that the fillings are robust and flavored well enough to stand out. Empanadas can be either baked or fried; baking is the lower-fat way of cooking them, and if you plan to rewarm them or serve them from a

warmer or chafing dish, this is the technique of choice. The crisp richness that frying in hot vegetable oil provides, however, is hard to resist.

1. Prepare the filling, cover, and refrigerate it while preparing the dough. Make the dough according to your chosen recipe and chill for at least 1 hour. Roll the dough out on a floured surface into an even rectangle about $1/16$ inch thick. For convenience, you may wish to cut the dough in half and roll it in 2 batches. Keep the cut dough covered and chilled while making the empanadas. Make sure to use enough flour to prevent the dough from sticking. "Shrink down" the dough by lifting it from the table with your fingers and letting it contract naturally. This will prevent the circles or squares from becoming misshapen as you cut them.

2. Cut the dough into the desired shape. For rounds, use either a round cookie cutter or an appropriately sized can as a guide for a paring knife. For squares, use a ruler to guide you. Allow the dough to rest, refrigerated, for 30 minutes or overnight, before filling.

3. Spoon the filling onto the center of each of 8 to 10 circles. Fold the first turnover to make sure that the amount of filling is correct for a properly filled turnover. Brush halfway around the edges of the pastry with egg wash or water and fold the dough over the filling.

4. Using your fingers, press firmly on the edges of the dough to form a tight seal. A fork that has been dipped in flour may be used to seal the edges extra well and to provide a decorative edge, but this step is not mandatory. If desired, the turnovers may be brushed with egg wash to help them take on a more golden patina when baked or fried. Repeat to fill and seal the remaining circles.

5. Place sealed empanadas on a baking sheet that has been lined with parchment paper or waxed paper. Refrigerate for at least 1 hour before cooking.

6. To fry empanadas, start by preheating the oven to 250° (so that you can keep finished empanadas warm). In a large, heavy pot or deep-fryer, heat 3 inches of corn oil or peanut oil to 375°, or until sizzling hot but not smoking. Fry 8 to 10 of the turnovers for 3 to 4 minutes, or until golden brown color, turning them as needed.

7. To bake empanadas, preheat the oven to 350° or to the temperature indicated in your recipe. Place the turnovers on a baking sheet that has been lined with parchment paper, or lightly oiled. Brush them with egg wash and bake them for 8 to 12 minutes, or until golden, or as instructed in your recipe.

8. Serve the empanadas at once. They may be plated and sauced with garnishes, streakers, or escabeche, or they may be served as hors d'oeuvres with an appropriate dipping sauce. If you are passing the empanadas as an hors d'oeuvre, let them cool slightly.

plantain empanadas

makes about 30 cocktail-sized empanadas

These are good hors d'oeuvres for passing or for buffets. The sweet, buttery plantains are the perfect contrast to the tropical-hot flavor of the Fire-Roasted Tomato and Scotch Bonnet Salsa. The operative word for success here is ripe. Starchy plantains will not incorporate into the dough and will add little if any charm to the filling. If you can't find dark-skinned plantains, use ripe bananas.

FOR THE DOUGH

3 cups all-purpose flour

1 1/4 cups cornmeal

1 1/2 teaspoons salt

1/3 cup (2/3 stick) cold butter, cut into 1/2-inch cubes

3/4 cup diced ripe plantain or banana

3 egg yolks

2 tablespoons sherry vinegar

1/4 to 1/2 cup water

FOR THE FILLING

1 large plantain, or 2 bananas

Juice of 2 limes

1/2 cup queso fresco or diced Muenster cheese, about 4 ounces

1 large jalapeño, diced

Salt and coarsely ground black pepper to taste

1 teaspoon milk

1 egg, slightly beaten

Corn or peanut oil for frying (optional)

2 cups Fire-Roasted Tomato and Scotch Bonnet Salsa (page 21), warmed

For the dough, stir the flour, cornmeal, and salt together in a medium bowl. Add the butter to the dry ingredients with the plantain. Using either a pastry cutter, your hands, or a heavy-duty mixer with a paddle attachment, cut the butter and banana into the dry ingredients until pea-sized pieces are formed. Do not overmix.

If mixing by hand, make a well in the center of the ingredients and add the egg yolks and vinegar. If using a mixer, add the yolks and vinegar gradually while the mixer runs on the lowest speed. Stir to just blend. Add the water and blend just until a soft dough forms. Small nuggets of fruit and butter should still be visible in the dough. Do not overmix. Form the dough into a $^3/_4$-inch-thick square, wrap, and refrigerate for 1 hour to overnight before rolling.

Let the dough sit at room temperature for 2 to 4 minutes, then roll it out on a floured surface into an even rectangle about $^1/_{16}$ inch thick. Shrink down the dough by lifting it off the table and allowing it to contract. Using a 3- to 4-inch round cutter, cut the dough into circles. If desired, cover them with plastic and chill for 1 hour or overnight.

For the filling, peel the plantain and cut it into $^1/_4$-inch dice. Put the plantain in a small bowl and stir in the lime juice right away. Add the remaining ingredients for the filling. Taste and adjust the seasoning, being careful not to overstir and mangle the filling.

Beat the milk into the egg to use as an egg wash to seal and brush the pastries. Spoon $1^1/_2$ teaspoons of the filling onto the center of each of 8 to 10 circles. Brush halfway around the edges of each circle with the egg wash and fold the dough over the filling. Press the edges of the dough to seal. Repeat to fill the remaining circles. Wrap and refrigerate the pastries for 1 to 4 hours before baking.

To bake the empanadas, preheat the oven to 350°. Place the empanadas on parchment-lined or lightly oiled baking sheets and bake for 8 to 12 minutes, or until browned and slightly crisp. To fry the empanadas, heat 3 inches of the oil to 350°, or until sizzling but not smoking, in a large, heavy pot or deep-fryer. Fry 8 to 10 empanadas at a time in the oil for 3 to 4 minutes, or until golden brown, turning as needed. Remove with a slotted spoon and drain on paper towels. Place on a wire rack or grill screen set on a baking sheet. Place the pan in the warm oven. Repeat the process to fry the remaining empanadas. Serve at once with the salsa.

barbecued duck empanadas

makes about 30 cocktail-sized empanadas

Roasted duck, barbecue sauce, and tangy cheese combine here to make a satisfying snack that you'll be popping into your mouth repeatedly. Stop that! These are for company! This is a way to use leftover duck, but if you want to start from scratch, see the recipe on page 70.

FOR THE DOUGH

4 cups all-purpose flour

1 $^1/_2$ teaspoons salt

1 tablespoon sugar

$^1/_4$ cup Jimmy the B's Wildcat Barbecue Spice Rub (page 43)

1 cup (2 sticks) cold butter, cut into $^3/_4$-inch cubes

1 egg, lightly beaten

$^1/_2$ cup water, plus a few drops more if needed

FOR THE FILLING

1 cup pulled and shredded cooked duck meat, about 2 legs (see page 70)

6 tablespoons Jay's Quick and Easy Barbecue Sauce (page 121) or a premium brand

1 teaspoon minced fresh rosemary

¹/₄ teaspoon ground pepper or to taste

¹/₄ cup queso fresco or crumbled fresh goat cheese

2 teaspoons milk

1 egg, beaten

Peanut or corn oil for frying (optional)

2 cups Jay's Quick and Easy Barbecue Sauce (page 121), a premium brand barbecue sauce, or Chile Seco Salsa (page 23), slightly warmed, for dipping

For the dough, stir the flour, salt, sugar, and spice rub together in a large bowl. If mixing by hand, make a well in the center of the dough and add the butter. Using a pastry cutter or your fingers, cut the butter into the flour until the pieces are the size of a pea. Or, use a heavy-duty mixer fitted with the paddle attachment to cut in the butter. Add the egg and ¹/₂ cup water and mix until just blended, adding a few drops more water if necessary to make a smooth dough. Small lumps of butter should still be visible in the dough. Form the dough into a flat rectangle, cover, and refrigerate for at least 1 hour or up to 3 days.

For the filling, put the meat in a small bowl and stir in all of the ingredients except the cheese until the meat is well coated. Taste and adjust the seasoning. Fold in the cheese until it is just well distributed. If making in advance, cover and refrigerate for up to 1 day.

Let the dough sit at room temperature for 2 to 3 minutes, then roll it out on a floured surface into an even rectangle about ¹/₁₆-inch thick. Shrink down the dough by lifting it off the table and allowing it to contract. Using a 3- to 4-inch round cutter, cut the dough into circles. If desired, cover them with plastic and chill for 30 minutes to overnight.

In a small bowl, beat milk into the egg and set aside. Place about 2 teaspoons of filling in the center of 8 to 10 circles and brush lightly halfway around the edges with the egg wash. Press the edges of the dough to seal. Brush the tops of the pastries with the egg wash. Repeat to fill and seal the remaining circles. Cover and refrigerate the empanadas for up to 24 hours before cooking.

To fry the empanadas, preheat the oven to 250°. Heat 3 inches of the oil to 350° in a large, heavy pot or deep-fryer. Drop in 8 to 10 cold empanadas and cook for 4 to 5 minutes, or until they are golden brown, turning as needed. Remove the empanadas with a slotted spoon and drain them on paper towels. Place them on a wire rack or grill screen set on a baking sheet and put the pan in the warm oven. Repeat to fry the remaining empanadas. To bake the empanadas, preheat the oven to 350°. Place them on a parchment paper–lined or lightly oiled baking sheet and bake for 7 to 8 minutes, or until golden brown. Serve with the barbecue sauce or chile salsa.

PULLED AND SHREDDED COOKED DUCK MEAT: Season 2 duck legs with a mixture of 1 teaspoon salt, 1 teaspoon chile molido, and ¹/₂ teaspoon freshly ground black pepper. Let sit for 1 hour, then roast in a 350° oven for 30 to 40 minutes, or until the meat can be pulled away from the bone without resistance. Let cool, then pull the meat from the bone and shred or dice it. Discard the bones and gristle.

pork carnitas empanadas

makes about 30 cocktail-sized empanadas

Carnitas is a traditional pork filling for the tacos and burritos sold at colorful roadside stands throughout Mexico. In its original incarnation, the meat was slowly cooked in lard until tender and crisp. This version calls for the meat to be covered in water and simmered until tender. The meat is then sautéed in its own minimal rendered fat until well browned. Not exactly health food, but a giant step in the right direction. This filling can also be used for rellenos and enchiladas.

FOR THE DOUGH

1¹/₂ cups cornmeal

3 cups all-purpose flour

1 tablespoon salt

Uncooked Pork Carnitas Empanadas (top left), Barbecued Duck Empanadas being prepared (upper right), Plantain Empanadas (bottom)

³/₄ cup (1 ¹/₂ sticks) cold butter, cut into ¹/₂-inch cubes

6 egg yolks

3 tablespoons cider vinegar

³/₄ cup water, plus a few drops more if needed

¹/₄ cup finely chopped fresh cilantro (optional)

FOR THE CARNITAS

1 pound pork butt, cut into 1-inch cubes

1 ¹/₄ cups water

1 ¹/₂ teaspoons chile caribe

3 cloves garlic, dry-roasted and coarsely chopped (see page 116)

3 tablespoons diced onion

³/₄ teaspoon ground cumin

³/₄ teaspoon dried Mexican oregano

1 teaspoon ground canela, or ¹/₂ teaspoon ground cinnamon

Pinch of ground allspice

FOR THE FILLING

Carnitas (above)

1 ¹/₂ cups (6 ounces) grated smoked mozzarella or Muenster cheese

¹/₂ cup fresh cilantro, coarsely chopped

2 large jalapeño chiles, diced

²/₃ cup Chile Seco Salsa (page 21) or Fire-Roasted Tomato and Scotch Bonnet Salsa (page 23)

2 teaspoons milk

1 egg

Peanut or corn oil for frying

2 cups Chile Seco Salsa (page 21) or Fire-Roasted Tomato and Scotch Bonnet Salsa (page 23), slightly warmed

For the dough, stir the cornmeal, flour, and salt together. Cut in the butter, using your fingers or a heavy-duty mixer fitted with a paddle attachment, until the mixture forms pea-sized pieces. Mix in the egg yolks and vinegar and until just blended. Add the ¹/₂ cup water and the cilantro and stir to form a soft dough. Add a few drops more water if needed. Do not overmix the dough. Press the dough into a flat rectangle, cover, and refrigerate for at least 1 hour, or up to 2 days.

For the carnitas, put the pork in a heavy pot with all the remaining carnitas ingredients. Bring the water to a simmer over moderate heat and cook the pork until it is tender and all the water has evaporated, about 30 to 40 minutes. Increase the heat slightly and sauté the meat until it is well browned. Pour it into a shallow pan to cool.

For the filling, dice the carnitas and stir them together with all the remaining ingredients until just well blended. Taste and adjust the seasoning. Cover and refrigerate.

Let the dough sit at room temperature for 2 to 3 minutes. On a floured surface, roll the dough out into an even rectangle about ¹/₁₆ inch thick. Shrink down the dough by lifting it off of the table and allowing it to contract. Using a 3- to 4-inch round cutter, cut the dough into circles. Beat the milk into the egg to make an egg wash. Spoon 2 teaspoons of the filling into the center of each dough circle. Brush halfway around the edges of each circle with the egg wash, fold the dough over the filling, seal, and crimp. If making in advance, cover and chill the empanadas for up to 24 hours.

To fry the empanadas, preheat the oven to 250°. Heat 3 inches of the oil to 350°, or until sizzling but not smoking, in a heavy pot or deep-fryer. Fry 10 to 12 empanadas at a time for 3 to 5 minutes, turning as needed, until golden brown. Using a slotted spoon, transfer the empanadas to paper towels to drain. Place the empanadas on a wire rack or grill screen set on a baking sheet and put the pan in the warm oven.

To bake the empanadas, preheat the oven to 350°. Place the pastries on a baking sheet lined with parchment paper or lightly oiled. Bake for 8 to 12 minutes, or until well browned and heated through. Serve at once with the salsa for dipping.

tamales

Nothing epitomizes the character, flavors, and traditions of the Southwest more than the ubiquitous tamale. Fragrant, steaming, and exploding with flavor, these wonderful bundles arrive at the table shrouded in a mist of fragrance and history. At least 450 years ago, the Aztecs were making these ground corn bundles in various forms and thought so highly of them that they were offered to the gods as part of elaborate religious celebrations. Today, tamales still bring a spirit of fiesta to parties and gatherings.

Although they are most often made with a filled dough made from masa harina, tamale doughs can be made from fresh corn, cooked potatoes, or grains such as quinoa. Some very satisfying and relatively effortless tamales are made by mixing a filling directly into the chosen dough instead of the layering and wrapping that is more common. Tamales are often wrapped in the dried corn husks found in Latino markets and many grocery stores, but they may also be wrapped in fresh corn husks or banana leaves, which impart a unique flavor of their own.

While well-made tamales help to define southwestern cooking at its best, they can also be intimidating to prepare. Rolling and tying that first tamale can seem like a daunting task if you have never seen anyone do it, but if you follow the directions on the following pages, you will feel like a seasoned tamale veteran.

1. To use dried corn husks, soak 1 husk per tamale, plus a few extras for tearing into strips for tying, in warm water, for 20 to 30 minutes. Weigh down the husks with a small plate to keep them submerged. Drain the rehydrated husks in a colander and lay them out on paper towels. Tear the extra husks into long, thin strips for tying. Prepare the tamale filling according to the recipe, cover, and refrigerate. Make the chosen dough and refrigerate or set it aside as instructed. To keep the tamales consistently sized, divide the dough into the stipulated number of portions and roll it into balls. Place a dough ball in the center of each husk or wrapper. Using your fingers, press the ball out into a rectangle almost to the sides of the husk, leaving about 1 1/2 inches uncovered at the tapered end and about 1/4 inch at the broad end.

2. Place the filling in a line down the center of the dough, leaving about a 1/4-inch margin at each end. For a tighter bundle, leave slightly more of the husk uncovered at the broad end and tie both ends. This method for rolling and tying tamales is both pretty and tasty. Other shapes and ties are discussed on page 74.

3. Take one long side of each wrapper and roll the dough around the filling as tightly as possible, making sure it seals around the filling. Take care not to roll the wrapper or corn husk into the center of the

tamale. If the corn husks are too small, lay the tamale over a second husk before rolling and tying.

4. Place the tamales seam-side down and, using one of the long, thin husk strips, tie the tapered end snugly where the dough and filling end. If necessary, pack the filling with your fingertips through the open end of the tamale to ensure a tight bundle.

5. When ready to cook, prepare a steamer by filling a large pot with at least 2 inches of water. Bring the water to a strong simmer over medium heat. Insert a steamer basket and add the tamales, being careful not to crowd them. If you are using bamboo baskets, leave the bottom one empty to keep the tamales from coming into contact with the wa-

ter. Cover the pot and steam the tamales for the time specified in the recipe, usually 10 to 20 minutes. The best doneness test for masa harina– and grain-based tamal doughs is to peel back the corn husk. If it peels away cleanly, the tamale is done. Fresh corn tamales will stick to the husks as they cook, and must be judged by either cooking time or by breaking one open. It is not unusual for tamales tied in the illustrated manner to ooze slightly out of the wrapper on the open end while cooking. If desired, you may trim them once they have rested. All tamales should rest for 5 minutes after steaming before being served. This allows for better texture and for the complete melding of flavors.

6. In addition to being wrapped in different wrappers, tamales can be tied into a variety of different shapes. When wrapped in banana leaves, they may be tied with string. For a festive look, try tying tamales with strips of cloth or colorful ribbons. Tamales can be served as hors d'oeuvres, appetizers, or light entrées.

what not to do

1. **If possible, avoid cooking masa harina–based doughs on the day that they are made. They will have a smoother, less cakelike texture if they are allowed to rest overnight in the refrigerator. They can be resoftened by being placed back in the mixer or food processor and mixed or whipped until light again, or the tamales may simply be made a day ahead.**

2. **Until you develop a sense for when they are truly done, make an extra tamale to break open so that you can check for doneness. More than one cook has been embarrassed by serving chalky tamales with not-quite-cooked shrimp or salmon inside.**

3. **Check the water level to be sure that the steamer does not boil dry, resulting in a scorched-tasting tamale. Conversely, make sure that there is sufficient space between the water level and the tamale to allow for even steaming.**

fresh corn tamales with chile caribe

makes 6 small tamales

Even before tamales were adopted by settler cooks in the Southwest, they were eaten elsewhere in North America. In 1612 in Virginia, Captain John Smith was served tamalli, *which were made from fresh corn that had been "bruised in a morter of wood, with a Polt" and wrapped in fresh corn husks. This simple recipe celebrates that first tamale encounter, and the fresh flavors and ease of preparation make this one good to serve as a side dish. Of course, fresh corn marries perfectly with seafood, and the addition of smoked salmon, shrimp, or crab would only add to this dish's allure and fragrance. In this recipe the filling and dough are combined.*

1 cup fresh corn kernels (about 1 large ear)

1 $^1/_2$ tablespoons butter at room temperature

$^1/_4$ cup yellow cornmeal

1 scant cup (4 ounces) grated Parmesan

$^1/_2$ cup (2 ounces) grated smoked mozzarella

1 egg white

$^1/_4$ teaspoon salt

$^1/_2$ teaspoon sugar

$^1/_4$ teaspoon ground black pepper

1 $^1/_2$ teaspoons coarsely chopped fresh basil or cilantro

1 teaspoon chile caribe

8 large fresh or dried corn husks, prepared for wrapping and tying (see page 73)

1 cup Fire-Roasted Tomatillo Salsa with Basil (page 23) or Fire-Roasted Tomato and Scotch Bonnet Salsa (page 21), slightly warmed (optional)

Put the corn kernels in a blender or food processor and pulse until well chopped. Add the butter and cornmeal and pulse until well blended. Add the cheeses and egg white and scrape down the sides of the container. Continue to pulse or chop just until a fairly smooth mixture is formed. Pour into a medium bowl and stir in the salt, sugar, pepper, basil, and chile caribe until blended. Taste and adjust the seasoning.

Lay the husks out on a work surface. Divide the corn mixture into 6 portions and roll each into a ball between your palms. Place a ball in the center of each husk. Press the mixture out into a rectangle almost to the sides of each husk, leaving 1$^1/_2$ inches uncovered at the tapered end and $^1/_4$ inch at the broad end. Take one long side of each husk and roll it around the mixture as tightly as possible. Place the tamale seam-side down and, using one of the long, thin husk strips, tie the tapered end snugly where the mixture ends. To prepare in advance, cover and refrigerate the tamales for up to 24 hours.

When ready to serve, steam the tamales over strongly simmering water in a covered pot for 10 to 12 minutes, or until a skewer inserted into the center comes out clean. Allow them to rest for about 5 minutes. Serve the tamales with one of the salsas, if desired.

smoked shrimp and basil tamales

makes 6 large tamales

Smoking the shrimp brings a hearty aroma to these elegant tamales that is worth the little bit of extra effort required to produce it. Of course, a perfectly tasty tamale can be made by simply marinating the seafood and eliminating the smoking step. The Barbecue Tamal Dough below is a good all-purpose dough that pairs well with most foods. It is also used for the crust in the Tamale Tarts on pages 80 and 82.

FOR THE BARBEQUE TAMAL DOUGH

6 tablespoons butter at room temperature

³/₄ cup masa harina

2 tablespoons yellow cornmeal

²/₃ teaspoon baking powder

³/₄ teaspoon salt

¹/₂ teaspoon sugar

2 teaspoons Chipotles en Adobo Purée (page 26)

5 tablespoons Jay's Quick and Easy Barbecue Sauce (page 121) or a premium brand

1 to 2 tablespoons water, if needed to yield a soft dough

FOR THE FILLING

12 medium shrimp or 24 small shrimp, peeled and deveined

¹/₂ cup Lime, Brown Sugar, and Hazelnut Oil Marinade (page 57), optional

8 corn husks prepared for wrapping and tying (see page 73)

6 large basil leaves

Smoked Shrimp and Basil Tamale served with Tomatillo and Pepper-Ring Escabeche, surrounded by a variety of different shapes and styles of tamale

6 tablespoons grated smoked mozzarella

6 teaspoons diced fire-roasted red pepper (see pages 18–19)

¹/₄ cup wood chips for smoking (optional)

1 ¹/₂ to 2 cups Fire-Roasted Tomatillo Salsa with Basil (page 21) or Chile Seco Salsa (page 23), optional, slightly warmed

For the tamal dough, place the butter in the bowl of an electric mixer or a food processor and beat or mix it until it is fluffy. Add the masa harina, baking powder, salt, and sugar, and mix them together until well blended. The mixture will be crumbly. Add the chipotle purée and barbecue sauce and mix or pulse until blended. Add water if necessary to make a dough that is soft but not sticky. If using a mixer, beat the dough at high speed for 10 to 12 minutes, or until it is light and fluffy. In a food processor, this consistency will be achieved in 6 to 8 minutes. To make in advance, cover and refrigerate for up to 3 days. Let the dough sit at room temperature for 5 to 10 minutes or beat it with a mixer on high speed to soften it before proceeding.

Put the shrimp in a nonreactive container. Stir in the marinade, cover, and refrigerate for 1 hour. If desired, hot-smoke the shrimp (see pages 54–55).

Divide the tamal dough into 6 portions and roll each into a ball between your palms. Place one ball of dough in the center of each husk and press it out with your fingertips into an even rectangle that reaches almost to the sides of the husk, leaving 1¹/₂ inches at the tapered end and ¹/₄ inch at the broad end. Lay 1 basil leaf over the center of the masa and top with 2 shrimp. Evenly divide the cheese and pepper over the seafood. Take one long side of each husk and roll the dough around the filling as tightly as possible. Place the tamales seam-side down and, using one of the long, thin strips, tie the tapered end snugly where the dough and filling end. To prepare in advance, cover and refrigerate for up to 24 hours.

When ready to serve, steam the chilled tamales over strongly simmering water in a covered pan for 18 to 20 minutes, or until a husk pulls away cleanly from the dough. Let the tamales rest for 5 minutes before serving. Serve the tamales with tomatillo or chile salsa, if desired.

spicy duck and banana tamales

makes 6 large tamales or 8 small ones

Like Plantain Empanadas (page 68), this recipe uses buttery fruit to replace some of the butter. In Central and South America, there are as many different types of bananas as there are apples in the Pacific Northwest, and several different kinds are now being exported. Red bananas, with their tropical mango and papaya overtones, would work very well in this recipe, as long as they are very ripe.

FOR THE TAMAL DOUGH

1 cup masa harina

2 tablespoons cornmeal

$^1/_2$ teaspoon baking powder

$^3/_4$ teaspoon salt

3 ounces ripe banana ($^1/_3$ cup packed)

$^1/_4$ cup butter, at room temperature

6 tablespoons Chile Seco Salsa (page 23) or
   Jay's Quick and Easy Barbeque Sauce (page 121).

FOR THE FILLING

1 large ripe banana

Juice of 1 lime

1 cup pulled and shredded cooked duck meat
   (about 2 legs) (see page 70)

$^1/_4$ cup scallion rings, green part only

$^1/_2$ cup (2 ounces) grated smoked mozzarella

2 teaspoons finely diced jalapeño (or to taste)

8 to 10 fresh or dried corn husks prepared for
   wrapping and tying (see page 73)

2 cups Chile Seco Salsa (page 23), slightly
   warmed (optional)

For the dough, put the masa harina, cornmeal, baking powder, and salt in the bowl of an electric mixer or food processor. Add the bananas and butter and mix together until smooth. Add the chile salsa and pulse or stir to blend. Beat the dough on high speed until it is light and fluffy, 8 to 10 minutes in a mixer, 5 to 6 minutes in a food processor. The dough may be made ahead, covered, and refrigerated for up to 3 days, but it should be brought back to room temperature or beaten in a mixer on high speed for a few minutes to soften it before proceeding.

Make the filling just before rolling the tamales. For the filling, peel and dice the banana. Put the banana in a medium bowl and pour the lime juice over it. Add all the remaining filling ingredients and gently stir to blend.

Divide the dough into 6 or 8 portions and roll each into a ball between your palms. Place 1 ball in the center of each husk. Press the dough out into a rectangle almost to the sides of the husk, leaving $1^1/_2$ inches uncovered at the tapered end and $^1/_4$ inch at the broad end. Place $^1/_6$ of the filling in a line down the center of the dough, leaving a $^1/_4$-inch margin at each end.

Take one long side of each husk and roll the dough around the filling as tightly as possible. Place the tamales seam-side down and, using one of the long, thin strips, tie the tapered end snugly where the dough and filling end. To prepare in advance, cover and refrigerate for up to 4 hours.

When ready to serve, steam the tamales over strongly simmering water in a covered pot for 12 to 20 minutes, depending on their size, or until a husk peels away cleanly from the dough. Allow the tamales to rest for 5 minutes before serving. Serve with the reserved chile sauce.

tamale tarts

Originally created by Stephan Pyles, tamale tarts combine the rustic flavors of dried chiles and tamal dough with a quichelike custard. These tarts now bring a touch of bucolic elegance to southwestern restaurants across the land, including Stephan's new Star Canyon. Once you have mastered the simple recipes provided here, you can create your own flavor combinations. As with quiche, you can either make a large one and cut it into wedges, or make an individual one for each guest. These tarts make great appetizers, or they can be paired with a small salad and served as a light entrée. Tamale tarts may be steamed like tamales for a softer consistency that more closely resembles a true tamale. For convenience, or for large tarts, the dough-lined shells may be blind-baked like quiches and pies. The custard and fillings can then be added and the tarts baked in the oven.

1. Prepare the tamal dough according to the recipe. Line a tart pan (or pans) with a removable bottom with a $1/8$-inch thickness of dough. If desired, from this point the tarts may be prepared like conventional quiches.

2. Make the custard as directed in the recipe. To ensure the even distribution of ingredients such as peppers, cheeses, and chopped herbs, divide them among the tarts before pouring in the custard. Pour the well-stirred custard to within $1/4$ inch of the top rim of the tart.

3. Carefully wrap the tarts in plastic, sealing them well. Place them in a steamer over 2 inches of strongly simmering water, being sure to keep the tarts flat. A bamboo steamer is a good choice. A wok with a round wire rack insert can also be used, as long as the rack stays well above the level of the water.

4. Cover the steamer and steam the tamales until the custard has set, about 10 to 12 minutes for small tarts, 15 to 20 for large ones. Let small tarts cool for at least 5 minutes, large ones for at least 10 minutes. Remove the tart(s) from the pan(s). Cut large tarts into wedges.

5. For light entrées or hearty appetizers, tamale tarts may be served with tossed greens, escabeches, or simply with salsas, sauces, or streakers.

what not to do

1. Don't steam tamale tarts over high heat. The water should remain at a strong simmer. Cooking the tarts too quickly may make the eggs in the custard scramble, giving the finished dish a lumpy or rubbery texture.

2. Don't line the tart shells with tamal dough the day before cooking. Most tart pans are not corrosion resistant and will rust or react with the acids in the dough, turning it black.

poblano and roasted-corn tamale tarts with rosemary

makes four 4-inch tarts

Who says vegetarian entrées have to be wimpy? The three major flavors combine here to make these taste memorable. For convenience, this recipe can be made into one 11-inch tart and cut into wedges. For a colorful and flavor-enhancing contrast, drizzle a little Fire-Roasted Tomato and Scotch Bonnet Salsa (page 21) around the finished tarts.

1 recipe Barbecue Tamal Dough (page 77)

1 ^{1}/$_4$ cups half-and-half

^{1}/$_3$ cup coarsely chopped fresh rosemary

1 poblano chile, fire-roasted, peeled, and diced (see pages 18–19)

^{3}/$_4$ cup chopped fresh cilantro

1 cup fresh corn kernels (1 large ear), dry-roasted (see page 116)

3 eggs

2 large cloves garlic, dry-roasted (see page 116)

1 ^{1}/$_2$ teaspoons salt

1 tablespoon sugar

Freshly ground black pepper to taste

6 tablespoons freshly grated Parmesan cheese

^{1}/$_2$ cup Grilled Onion (page 51)

^{1}/$_2$ cup diced roasted red bell pepper (see pages 18–19)

Prepare the dough and divide it into 4 equal portions. Press the dough into the sides and bottoms of four 4-inch tart pans to an ^{1}/$_8$-inch thickness. To bake the tarts, line the pans with parchment paper or aluminum foil and fill them with pie weights, rice, or dried beans and bake the shells in a preheated 350° oven for 8 to 12 minutes, or until the dough is set. Reduce the oven heat to 325°.

Put the half-and-half in a small saucepan with the rosemary and bring it to a boil. Remove from the heat immediately and let the liquid cool for 10 minutes. Strain the half-and-half and discard the rosemary. Place half of the diced poblano, half of the cilantro, and half of the corn in a blender and pour the half-and-half mixture over it. Blend until smooth. Pour the mixture into a medium bowl and whisk in the eggs, garlic, salt, sugar, and pepper.

Divide the remaining ingredients evenly among the tart shells and pour the custard to within ^{1}/$_4$ inch of the rim of each shell. If baking the tarts, place them in the 325° oven for 30 to 40 minutes, or until the custard has set. If steaming the tarts, wrap them well in plastic wrap and steam them over strongly simmering water in a covered pot for 20 to 30 minutes, or until the custard has set. Allow the tarts to rest for 5 minutes before turning them out of the pans and serving.

Poblano and Roasted-Corn Tamale Tart with Rosemary topped with Dry-Roasted Corn and Sweet Pepper Salsa (top left), Smoked Salmon and Spinach Tamale Tart (bottom)

smoked salmon and spinach tamale tart

makes one 11-inch tart or four 4-inch tarts

This very pretty and satisfying dish makes a perfect appetizer or light entrée. Infusing the milk and cream with the smoked salmon before making the custard brings out the full flavor of the delicate fish. You can use the trim and tail pieces left over from sliced salmon if you like. Serve the tart with a simple salad and a smile.

1 recipe Barbecue Tamal Dough (page 77)

1^1/$_2$ cups half-and-half

3 ounces smoked salmon, diced

2 teaspoons olive oil

3 large shallots, sliced into very thin rings

4 cloves garlic, sliced thin

Minced zest of 1 lemon

6 cups packed fresh spinach

1 tablespoon water

^{1}/$_2$ cup grated manchego or Parmesan cheese

1 guajillo chile, stemmed, seeded, and minced

3 eggs

2 egg yolks

^{3}/$_4$ teaspoon salt

^{1}/$_4$ teaspoon ground pepper

Prepare the dough and press it onto the bottom and sides of the tart pan to a ^{1}/$_8$-inch thickness. To bake the tart, preheat the oven to 350°. Line the pan with parchment paper or aluminum foil and fill it with pie weights, rice, or dried beans. Bake the shell for 8 to 12 minutes, or until the dough has set. Reduce the oven temperature to 325°.

In a small saucepan, heat the half-and-half just to the simmering point. Remove from the heat and stir in the smoked salmon. Let set for 5 to 10 minutes.

Meanwhile, in a large sauté pan or skillet over medium-high heat, heat the olive oil and sauté the shallot rings and garlic until golden brown, about 1 minute, stirring just enough to prevent burning. Add the lemon zest and sauté for another 30 seconds. Add the spinach and sauté until the spinach is just completely wilted, adding the water if needed to prevent scorching. (It is easier to do this in 2 batches.) Spread the cooked spinach out in a shallow pan and let it cool. Squeeze the spinach by handfuls to extract as much water as possible. Chop the spinach coarsely.

Arrange the spinach over the bottom of the tart shell. Drain the salmon well and distribute it over the spinach, reserving the half-and-half. Sprinkle the cheese and guajillo over the salmon.

In a medium bowl, whisk the reserved half-and-half, eggs, and egg yolks together to blend. Stir in the salt and pepper. Pour the mixture into the tart shell to just within ^{1}/$_4$ inch of the rim. To bake the tart, place it into the 325° oven and bake for 30 to 40 minutes, or until the custard has set. To steam the tart, wrap it in plastic wrap, sealing it well. Steam the tart over strongly simmering water in a covered steamer for 25 to 30 minutes, or until the custard is set. Let cool for 5 to 10 minutes before removing the tart from the pan, slicing, and serving.

flautas

lautas, or "little flutes," are corn tortillas that have been softened in hot oil or lard, filled with one of a variety of fillings, rolled into a narrow tube, and then fried until crisp. They are traditionally served on lettuce or slaw, and the contrast of crunchy outer tortilla against the soft fillings is a true delight. The secret to flauta joy is to serve them very fresh and hot, as soon as they have cooled enough to eat. In Mexico, anything that is rolled in a tortilla is called a taco. This simple fact has led to much confusion for diners on both sides of the border. Technically, enchiladas, flautas, cushions, and a variety of other foods could be, and have been, labeled as tacos. Those U-shaped corn tortillas filled with hamburger, which are impossible to eat without leaving "souvenirs" on your clothing, are an American bastardization that bears little similarity to any true Mexican or southwestern dish.

Yes, fried foods are a guilty indulgence. But no one expects you to make a steady diet of these, and flautas are a great way to give yourself an occasional treat.

1. Prepare the filling according to the recipe, cover, and refrigerate. Place the tortillas flat on a large surface in a single layer for 3 to 4 minutes, or until they are leathery but not brittle. In a shallow pan, heat 1 inch of oil to 325°, or until it sizzles but doesn't smoke. Immerse 1 tortilla in the oil for 1 or 2 seconds. Using tongs, transfer each tortilla to paper towels to drain, blotting the surface to remove excess oil.

2. While the tortillas are still soft, spoon some of the filling in a line down the center of a tortilla. Roll into a cylinder as snugly and tightly as possible without allowing it to tear. Some of them will split, so always prepare a few extra tortillas. "Sew" the seam closed with a toothpick. With your fingers, pack the filling in on each end of the tortilla to keep it from spilling. Repeat to roll and seal the remaining softened tortillas. Loosely cover the filled tortillas. If the filling is relatively dry, the flautas may be prepared to this point up to 24 hours in advance.

3. When ready to serve the flautas, heat 3 to 4 inches of oil in a heavy pot to 375° or until sizzling hot but not smoking. Using tongs, add the filled tortillas carefully and cook them for 2 to 3 minutes, or until golden and quite crisp, turning them as needed. Using tongs, transfer the flautas to paper towels to drain. Place them on a wire rack or grill screen on a baking sheet. Place the baking sheet in the oven to

keep the flautas warm. Repeat the process to cook the remaining filled tortillas. Remove the toothpicks and serve immediately.

what not to do

1. **Don't cook too many flautas at once. This will lower the temperature of the oil, resulting in soggy and oily flautas.**

2. **Make sure to let tortillas dry for 3 or 4 minutes, or until they are leathery but not brittle, before dipping them in oil for flautas or any other dish. This keeps them from becoming greasy or soaking up oil.**

3. **Make sure that the tortillas are rolled very tightly and sealed well. If the filling spills into the oil, it will burn, shortening the life of the oil.**

wild mushroom and goat cheese flautas

makes 8 flautas

These wonderful little flutes have been a Red Sage standard for years, and they are almost always on the menu in some incarnation. Whether served over spicy slaw and circled with Chile Seco Salsa (page 23) or as a side dish for grilled steaks or game, this is one of those outstanding dishes that fits squarely in the "Don't you dare change that recipe!" column.

FOR THE FILLING

3 tablespoons butter

1 ¹/₂ tablespoons vegetable oil

12 ounces mushrooms (creminis, portobellos, shiitakes, etc.), sliced

4 packed cups Swiss chard leaves, blanched, and squeezed, coarsely chopped

2 teaspoons minced serrano chile

1 teaspoon minced garlic

2 teaspoons minced fresh marjoram

1 teaspoon minced fresh oregano

1 tablespoon Chipotles en Adobo Purée (page 26)

¹/₂ teaspoon salt or to taste

¹/₂ teaspoon ground black pepper or to taste

¹/₄ cup fresh goat cheese

¹/₂ cup grated Monterey jack cheese

Eight 8-inch corn tortillas

Peanut or corn oil for frying

Preheat the oven to 250°. In a large sauté pan or skillet over medium-high heat, melt the butter with the oil and sauté the mushrooms, stirring occasionally, for 5 to 8 minutes, or until well browned and cooked through. Pour the mushrooms into a sieve and press on them lightly with the back of a large spoon. Place the mushrooms in a bowl with all the remaining filling ingredients and stir to mix well. Taste and adjust the seasoning.

Lay the tortillas on a flat surface in a single layer for 3 to 4 minutes, or until they are leathery but not brittle. Heat 1 inch of oil in a skillet to 325°, or until it is hot but not sizzling. Place 1 tortilla in the oil for 1 to 2 seconds, or until it is pliable. Using tongs, place the tortilla on a paper towel to drain. Repeat this step with the remaining tortillas. Drain them well, blotting the surfaces to take away excess oil. The flautas may be prepared to this point up to 24 hours in advance, but they must be covered airtight with plastic wrap to keep them from drying out or cracking. Refrigerate until ready to serve.

When ready to serve, heat 3 to 4 inches of oil to 375°, or until sizzling hot but not smoking, in a large, heavy pot or deep-fryer. Using tongs, put 2 to 4 flautas in the hot oil and fry them, turning as needed, for 3 to 5 minutes, or until they are golden and crisp. Using tongs, transfer the flautas to a baking sheet lined with paper towels. Place the flautas on a wire rack or grill screen set on a baking sheet. Put the pan in the warm oven. Repeat this process to cook the remaining flautas. Remove the toothpicks and serve the flautas at once.

apple, walnut, and bacon flautas with blue cheese

makes 6 flautas

This classic combination of flavors is greatly enhanced by a little touch of "cowboy cuisine." Serve these just as they are for noshing, or serve them on salad greens that have been tossed in a light sherry or red wine vinaigrette. Sacré bleu, podna!

FOR THE FILLING

3 to 4 slices bacon

3 Granny Smith or other tart green apples, peeled, cored, and diced

1 1/2 teaspoons fresh thyme

1/4 teaspoon ground black pepper

Juice of 1 lime

2 teaspoons packed brown sugar or to taste

1/4 cup walnuts, toasted and coarsely chopped (see page 117)

1 cup (4 ounces) crumbled blue cheese or aged goat cheese

Six 8-inch yellow or blue corn tortillas

For the filling, cook the bacon in a large sauté pan or skillet over medium heat until the fat has rendered and the bacon is brown but not crisp, about 3 to 5 minutes. Using a slotted spoon, remove the bacon, leaving the fat in the pan. Sauté the apples in the bacon fat, stirring gently, for 6 to 8 minutes, or until evenly browned and tender, but not mushy. Add the thyme and remove the apples from the heat. Add the pepper, lime juice, and brown sugar and stir well. Pour the apple mixture into a shallow pan and spread it out to cool to room temperature. Put the cool apple mixture into a medium bowl and stir in the bacon, walnut, and cheese.

Lay the tortillas on a flat surface in a single layer for 3 to 4 minutes, or until they are leathery but not brittle. Heat 1 inch of oil in a skillet to 325°, or until it is hot but not sizzling. Place 1 tortilla in the oil for 1 to 2 seconds, or until it is pliable. Using tongs, place the tortilla on a paper towel to drain. Repeat this step with the remaining tortillas. Drain them well, blotting the surfaces to take away excess oil. Spoon about 4 tablespoons of the filling in a line down the center of a tortilla and roll it into a tight cylinder. Close the seam with a toothpick. Repeat to roll and seal the remaining tortillas. The flautas may be prepared to this point up to 24 hours in advance, but they must be covered airtight with plastic wrap to keep them from drying or splitting. Refrigerate the flautas until ready to serve them.

When ready to serve the flautas, heat 3 to 4 inches of oil to 375°, or until sizzling but not smoking, in a large, heavy pot or deep-fryer. Using tongs, add 3 or 4 flautas to the oil and fry for 3 to 5 minutes, or until golden and crisp. Using tongs, transfer the flautas to a baking sheet lined with paper towels. Place the flautas on a wire rack or grill screen set on a baking sheet. Put the pan in the warm oven. Repeat the process to fry the remaining flautas. Remove the toothpicks and serve the flautas at once. If you like, cut the flautas in half on the diagonal with a serrated knife before serving.

Apple, Walnut, and Bacon Flautas with Blue Cheese

enchiladas

nchilar means to coat in chiles. Some simple recipes for traditional enchiladas call for corn tortillas to be passed through a chile purée, then fried briefly, searing the purée onto the surface and rendering the tortillas pliable enough to roll. These enchiladas are served accompanied with little more than Mexican crema. More elaborate traditional recipes call for tortillas to be briefly fried, then dipped in sauce. The tortillas are then filled with cheese, warm carnitas, or any of an endless variety of other fillings and rolled into cylinders. The same sauce is usually poured over them, and a garnish is added. Although some recipes call for enchiladas to be made ahead and baked, this can yield soggy tortillas and the practice isn't recommended. These rich, hearty concoctions make satisfying casual appetizers and entrées.

And from the *Jean-Louis Meets Cowboy Bob* file come some subtle and delicate recipes that use crepes instead of tortillas. Although they are not technically enchiladas, they are lighter and do not require the heavy dosing of sauces that traditional recipes sometimes call for. Even though we have borrowed the method from our French brethren, we have replaced the cream and milk with beer and usually add chile molido or puréed poblanos for color and spice.

tortilla method

1. For tortilla-wrapped enchiladas, make the filling and sauce according to the recipe and keep them warm. Air-dry the tortillas for 3 or 4 minutes, until they are leathery but not brittle. Preheat the oven to 250°. In a shallow pan, heat 1 inch of oil to 375°, or until it sizzles but doesn't smoke. Dip the tortillas one by one into the hot oil for 1 or 2 seconds and drain them on paper towels. Dip the tortillas in the sauce and allow them to drain, leaving a light coating of sauce.

2. Working quickly, spoon a line of filling down the center of the tortilla and roll it into a tight cylinder. Put the enchilada on its serving dish seam-side down and repeat the process until all enchiladas are rolled. When ready to serve, ladle some sauce over the enchiladas and garnish as desired.

crepe method

1. For crepe-wrapped enchiladas, make the fillings and sauces according to the recipe. Unlike the tortilla-wrapped enchiladas, these can either be made with warm ingredients and served right away, or made ahead and reheated for convenience. If reheating, cover and refrigerate the filling for 1 hour to overnight before rolling or filling the crepes. Lay the crepes out on a work surface and spoon 3 to 4 tablespoons of the filling in a line down the center for rolled crepes or in a dollop in the center for folded crepes. Roll the crepes into cylinders or fold them into square parcels. If not serving them right

away, place them seam-side down on their serving platter and keep them warm in a preheated 250° oven. If the crepes are being made ahead, cover and refrigerate them until serving time.

2. If reheating crepe-wrapped enchiladas, place the crepes seam-side down on a buttered or parchment paper–lined baking sheet and cover them with buttered aluminum foil. When ready to serve, preheat the oven to 300° and heat the crepes for 25 to 35 minutes, or until warmed through. To microwave, place them on a microwavable plate, cover with plastic wrap, and heat on medium for 1 minute, or until hot.

3. Sauce and garnish the crepes as desired. As with traditional enchiladas, this is usually done by saucing, then streaking them with crema and perhaps topping them with a dollop of salsa.

what not to do

1. **As when making flautas, make sure that the corn tortillas are air-dried, but not to the point of being brittle. Otherwise, they may become too crisp to roll without tearing. Conversely, if they are too fresh and soft, they will take on too much oil and repel the sauce.**

2. **Although it is inadvisable to bake enchiladas, the filling can sometimes grow cold while you are rolling the tortillas. In a pinch, try "zapping" them in the microwave for a few seconds to get them piping hot again before serving.**

smoked turkey and grilled onion enchiladas with red sauce

makes 8 enchiladas; serves 4 as an entrée

In Mexico, enchiladas are often relegated to street stalls and coffee shops, having been deemed too common for inclusion on the menus of better restaurants. That's a pity, because they provide a broad canvas on which to paint with some vivid colors. This rustic dish has the added bonus of providing a use for the leftover leg and thigh meat from smoked or roasted turkey.

1 $^1/_2$ tablespoons olive oil

4 large cloves garlic, chopped

Minced or grated zest of $^1/_2$ lime

5 cups coarsely chopped stemmed red chard, about 1 bunch

1 tablespoon water

2 cups diced smoked or roasted turkey, preferably dark meat

1 cup Grilled Onion (page 51), diced

1 $^1/_2$ to 2 tablespoons Chipotles en Adobo Purée (page 26)

1 $^1/_2$ teaspoons salt or to taste

$^1/_2$ teaspoon ground pepper or to taste

Eight 8-inch corn tortillas

Vegetable oil for the tortillas

Red Sauce (recipe follows)

1 cup (4 ounces) grated Monterey jack or Muenster cheese

$^1/_2$ cup Crema (page 101), optional

1 cup Salsa Fresca (page 34), well drained, optional

$^1/_4$ cup fresh cilantro leaves

In a large sauté pan or skillet over medium-high heat, heat half of the olive oil and sauté the garlic for 2 to 3 minutes, or until lightly browned. Add the lime zest and cook for 30 seconds, stirring constantly. Add the chard and cook the chard for a minute or so until it has wilted but is still bright green, adding the water if needed to prevent scorching the greens. Pour into a sieve to drain, then spread the chard out in a shallow pan to cool to the touch. Squeeze the chard by handfuls to remove the excess moisture. Cover and refrigerate.

In a large sauté pan or skillet over medium-high heat, heat the olive oil and sauté the turkey for 3 to 4 minutes, or until browned. Add the grilled onion, chipotle purée, and chard and salt and pepper. Reduce the heat to medium and sauté for 2 to 3 minutes, or until hot. Taste and adjust the seasoning. Set aside in a warm place. Prepare the Red Sauce and keep warm.

Preheat oven to 250°. Lay the tortillas on a flat surface and allow them to dry for 3 to 5 minutes, or until they are leathery but not brittle. Heat 1 inch of oil in a heavy skillet to 350°, or until it is sizzling hot but not smoking. Place one tortilla in the oil for 1 or 2 seconds, or until it is pliable. Remove the tortilla from the oil with tongs, and blot it on a paper towel. Pass the tortilla through the warm sauce to coat it lightly. Place the tortilla on a plate and portion $^1/_8$ of the filling and 1 tablespoon of the cheese down the center. Roll the enchilada into a tight cylinder. Hold the enchiladas in a warm oven while preparing the remainder. When ready to serve, place the enchiladas on 4 warm serving plates and pour some of the remaining sauce over them. Garnish with a sprinkling of the remaining cheese, a few ribbons of crema, and mounds of salsa, if desired. Sprinkle the cilantro leaves over the salsa and serve at once.

red sauce

makes 2 cups

3 ancho chiles and 2 guajillo chiles, stemmed, seeded, and toasted (see page 24)

1 tablespoon rendered duck fat or peanut oil

1 small yellow onion, diced

3 large cloves garlic, dry-roasted (see page 116)

3 Roma tomatoes, fire-roasted (see pages 18–19)

$1/2$ teaspoon cumin seeds, toasted (see page 117)

$1/4$ teaspoon dried Mexican oregano or regular oregano

2 cups water or Chicken Stock (page 122)

$1/2$ teaspoon salt

$1/4$ teaspoon sugar, if needed

Fresh lime juice to taste

Put the chiles in a medium bowl and add water to cover them. Soak for 20 minutes, then drain.

In a small sauté pan or skillet over medium heat, heat 1 teaspoon of the duck fat or oil and sauté the onion for 2 to 5 minutes, or until browned. Put the onion, roasted garlic, and tomatoes in a blender. Add the cumin, oregano, chiles, and 1 cup of the chicken stock. Purée until quite smooth. Add the salt and the sugar, if needed. Add enough of the remaining 1 cup chicken stock to make a sauce the consistency of light tomato sauce. Strain the sauce.

In a large sauté pan or skillet over medium heat, heat the sauce for 3 to 5 minutes. Add the lime juice, and taste and adjust the seasoning. Keep sauce warm over hot water until needed. This sauce can be made up to 2 days ahead and re-heated.

roasted portobello and marinated pepper enchiladas in red chile crepes

makes 8 enchiladas; serves 4 as an entrée

Okay, so you wouldn't find this enchilada in a market stall in Michoacán. But it is a very satisfying vegetarian entrée. The colorful crepes make a memorable presentation, and many of the elements of this dish may be prepared in advance.

FOR THE FILLING

4 large portobello mushrooms, stemmed and dark ribs removed

1 cup Herb Marinade for Grilled Vegetables (page 52)

2 *each* red bell peppers, yellow bell peppers, and poblano chiles, roasted, peeled, seeded, and cut into $^1/_4$-inch dice (see pages 18–19)

1 tablespoon sherry vinegar

1 $^1/_2$ teaspoons fresh lemon juice

Salt to taste

2 cups (8 ounces) grated Monterey jack or Muenster cheese

FOR THE CREPES

2 egg yolks

1 cup beer

$^1/_3$ cup all-purpose flour

$^1/_4$ cup cornmeal

$^3/_4$ teaspoon salt

$^1/_2$ teaspoon sugar

2 teaspoons chile molido

1 $^1/_2$ teaspoons butter, melted

1 $^1/_2$ to 2 cups Fire-Roasted Tomato and Scotch Bonnet Salsa (page 21) or Fire-Roasted Tomatillo Salsa with Basil (page 23), slightly warmed

$^1/_2$ cup Crema (page 101), optional

For the filling, preheat the oven to 400°. Brush the portobellos liberally with the marinade, put them on a baking sheet, and bake for 12 to 14 minutes, or until they are crisp and cooked through. Set aside to cool.

In a medium bowl, stir the pepper and poblano strips and the remaining marinade together. Let sit at room temperature for 30 minutes to 1 hour.

Cut the portobellos into $^1/_4$-inch dice. Drain the peppers and chiles well and stir them together with the mushrooms. Add the vinegar, lemon juice, and salt and stir. Fold in the cheese until well blended. To prepare in advance, cover and refrigerate up to 24 hours.

For the crepes, put the egg yolks in a bowl and whisk in the beer. In another bowl, stir together the flour, cornmeal, salt, sugar, and chile molido. Make a well in the center of the dry ingredients and pour in the egg mixture in a steady stream while whisking. Stir in the butter and blend well.

Spray a nonstick crepe pan or skillet with vegetable-oil cooking spray or brush it lightly with melted butter and heat over medium heat. Ladle in about $^1/_4$ cup of the crepe batter and tilt the pan quickly to coat the bottom of the pan. Return the crepe to the heat and cook for 1 to 2 minutes, or until it takes on an orange peel texture, browns around the edges, and pulls away from the sides of the pan. Using a metal spatula, turn the crepe and cook it for 30 seconds to 1 minute on the second side. Turn the crepe out onto a rack or parchment paper and let it cool completely. Repeat to cook the remaining batter.

Lay the crepes out on a work surface. Spoon $^1/_2$ cup of the filling in a line down the center of each crepe. Roll the crepes into cylinders. Place them seam-side down on warm serving plates and drizzle the salsa or sauce around them. Garnish with the crema if desired and serve at once.

Roasted Portobello and Marinated Pepper Enchiladas in Red Chile Crepes (top), Smoked Turkey and Grilled Onion Enchiladas with Red Sauce (bottom)

chorizo and potato enchiladas in blue corn tortillas

makes 8 enchiladas; serves 4 as an entrée

Spicy sausage, onions, and well-browned potatoes are a recurring combination in southwestern and Mexican cooking, and this recipe proves that it is indeed one of the best. Our recipe for chorizo (page 122) replaces some of the fat and pork found in traditional chorizo with lean chicken. It makes a delicious sausage that is not too spicy. If you don't have the means or time to make your own, use a good commercial brand; just make sure that it is well drained before adding it to the potatoes.

10 medium-sized red potatoes

2 cups homemade chorizo (page 122) or a premium brand, removed from casings

2 tablespoons olive oil

1 large onion, diced

Salt to taste

Eight 8-inch blue corn tortillas

Vegetable oil for frying the tortillas

Red Sauce (page 91)

$3/4$ cup (3 ounces) grated Monterey jack or Muenster cheese

$1/2$ cup scallion rings, green part only

$1/2$ cup fresh cilantro leaves

$1/2$ cup Crema (page 101), optional

1 cup Salsa Fresca (page 34), optional

For the filling, put the potatoes in a medium saucepan, add lightly salted water to cover, and bring the water to a boil. Reduce the heat to a simmer and cook the potatoes until they are cooked but still firm, about 15 to 20 minutes. Drain the potatoes in a colander and let them cool slightly. While they are still warm, peel and cut the potatoes into $1/2$-inch dice. Set aside.

In a large, heavy skillet, cook the chorizo until the fat has rendered and the meat has slightly browned, about 5 minutes. Drain the sausage, discarding the fat. Break the meat into $1/2$-inch chunks or chop it coarsely with a knife.

In a large cast-iron or nonstick skillet over medium-high heat, heat the olive oil and sauté the potatoes for 2 to 4 minutes, or until lightly browned, stirring as little as possible. Add the onion and cook until it is translucent and the potatoes are well browned, 3 to 5 minutes. Stir in the chorizo and cook until heated through. Taste the filling and add salt as needed. Prepare the Red Sauce and keep warm.

Preheat oven to 250°. Lay the tortillas on a flat surface and allow them to dry for 3 or 4 minutes, or until they are leathery but not brittle. Heat 1 inch of oil in a heavy skillet to 350°, or until it is sizzling hot but not smoking. Place one tortilla into the oil for 1 or 2 seconds, or until it is pliable. Using tongs, remove the tortilla and blot it on a paper towel. Pass it through the warm sauce to coat it lightly.

Spoon $1/8$ of the filling in a line down the center of each tortilla. Divide the cheese, scallions, and cilantro evenly over the filling. Roll the enchiladas into tight cylinders. Place the enchiladas seam-side down on warm serving plates and pour some of the sauce around. If desired, streak the enchiladas with crema and top them with a spoonful of salsa. Serve at once.

quesadillas

Quesadillas, the quintessential appetizer, can be a casual nosh with a frosty beer, or a fancy hors d'oeuvre filled with luxurious and elegant ingredients. Even at cocktail parties where eight to ten different varieties of elegant canapés and elaborate hors d'oeuvres are served, the question always remains the same: "Uhhh—yagotanymorequesadillas?" No matter what the occasion, these are such great crowd pleasers that you usually can't make them fast enough.

When ordering a quesadilla in Mexico, you are far more likely to be served what we would call an empanada. Corn or flour tortilla doughs are pressed out into circles, filled with queso fresco, spicy pork, or vegetables, then sealed into turnovers. They are then either baked on a *comal*, or griddle, without any added lard or oil, or fried in hot oil until crisp and hot. The name can be misleading in another way: *queso* means cheese, but many traditional "quesadilla" fillings contain none. In the Tex-Mex version, flour tortillas are covered with grated or crumbled cheeses and often with other fillings such as vegetables, smoked chicken, or barbecued beef, and either folded over or topped with another tortilla. They are then griddle-baked with minimal butter or oil and cut into wedges. Cremas and salsas added just before serving add to the sensory overload that makes quesadillas so addicting.

1. Grate the cheeses and prepare any fillings according to your recipe. Preheat the oven to 250°. Heat a griddle or a large sauté pan or skillet over medium heat and cook 2 tortillas, one at a time, for 5 to 10 seconds on each side to make them pliable. Lay the tortillas out on a work surface and sprinkle a layer of cheese over half of each tortilla, leaving a $1/2$-inch margin at the outer edge. Sprinkle any fillings over the cheese, leaving the same $1/2$-margin. Top the filling with another layer of cheese to keep the filling from soaking the tortilla. For passed hors d'oeuvres, the entire surface of the tortilla may be covered with cheese, the filling, and more cheese, then topped with a second tortilla. Use less cheese and filling to make thinner quesadillas. Cut them into small wedges.

2. Fold each tortilla over the filling and press lightly to flatten. Although they may be cooked in oil or sautéed dry in a nonstick skillet, the best-colored and crispest tortilla is achieved by brushing the surface of the tortilla very lightly with melted butter. You may prepare them up to this point

3 to 4 hours in advance, or if the fillings are fairly dry, overnight. If stacking them for storage, place parchment or waxed paper between each quesadilla to prevent them from sticking. Cover them airtight with plastic wrap and refrigerate. Let the quesadillas come to room temperature before cooking them. Heat a griddle or a large skillet over medium heat and cook a quesadilla for 2 or 3 minutes on each side, or until golden brown and crisp. Using a metal spatula, transfer the quesadilla to a baking sheet or grill screen. Put the pan in the warm oven. Repeat the process to cook the remaining quesadillas.

3. To serve, quickly transfer each quesadilla to a cutting board and cut it into 3 or more even wedges. Arrange the wedges

on a warm platter or plate and garnish with crema and an appropriate salsa. Serve at once.

what not to do

1. **Don't use high heat. If the temperature of the griddle or pan is too high, the tortilla will brown before the fillings are hot. Quesadillas may be heated through in the oven, but they are at their best cooked on a griddle or in a skillet and served as quickly as possible, when the contrast between the crisp tortilla, soft cheese, and moist filling is at its greatest.**

2. **If you are using a moist filling such as barbecued beef or pork, be sure to drain it well, so as not to soak the tortilla. While plain cheese quesadillas may be filled 1 day ahead, moister varieties should be made as close to serving time as possible.**

barbecued beef quesadillas

makes 4 quesadillas

In the kitchens of the Red Sage, where they sell about a zillion of these a week, whole briskets are placed in the computer-controlled smoker and barbecued for thirteen hours until they are redolent with an intoxicating smokiness. On the off chance that your computer-controlled smoker is on the fritz, or you don't want to wait thirteen hours before whipping up a hearty quesadilla, this easy alternative is offered for the home cook.

1 1/2 pounds beef top sirloin steak

2 tablespoons Jimmy the B's Wildcat Barbecue Spice Rub (page 43), or salt and pepper to taste

1 cup Jay's Quick and Easy Barbecue Sauce (page 121) or a premium brand

Four 10-inch flour tortillas

5 cups (10 ounces) grated Monterey jack or Muenster cheese

4 tablespoons butter at room temperature

OPTIONAL GARNISHES

1/2 cup Crema (page 101)

2 cups Salsa Fresca (page 34), drained

1/4 cup diagonally cut scallion rings, green part only

4 fresh cilantro sprigs

Prepare a fire in a charcoal or gas grill. Rub the meat with the spice rub or salt and pepper. Grill the meat over medium heat for at least 10 to 12 minutes, turning the meat twice. Let the meat rest for 5 minutes, then slice it very thinly across the grain.

Put the barbecue sauce in a medium saucepan, bring it to a low simmer, and stir in the meat along with any cutting juices. Stir to coat the meat and simmer it for 6 to 8 minutes, or until it is tender and well flavored. Pour the mixture into a shallow pan and let it cool.

Just before cooking, preheat the oven to 250°. Heat a griddle, large sauté pan, or large skillet over medium heat and cook 2 tortillas, one at a time, for 5 to 10 seconds on each side to make them pliable.

Portion 1/8 of the cheese over the bottom half of each tortilla, leaving a 1/2-inch margin around the edges. Place 1/4 of the filling over the cheese on each tortilla. Arrange the remaining cheese over the filling, maintaining the 1/2-inch margin around the edges. Fold the tortilla over the filling and press gently. Brush the tops of the quesadillas with half of the butter and place them on the griddle or in the pan, buttered side down. Reduce the heat to medium and brush the remaining butter over the quesadillas. Cook them for 2 or 3 minutes, or until they are crisp and golden brown. Using a spatula, turn the quesadillas carefully and cook them on the other side for another 2 or 3 minutes. It may be necessary to cook the quesadillas in 2 batches, holding the cooked ones on a baking sheet in the oven while cooking the remainder.

Cut the quesadillas into wedges and divide them among the warm serving plates. Streak the quesadillas with the crema, top with a mound of salsa, and sprinkle the scallions and cilantro over. Serve at once.

oven-dried tomato, mushroom, and roasted-garlic quesadillas

makes 4 quesadillas

In this "Muchachos on the Mediterranean" recipe, oven-dried tomatoes and basil leaves give quesadillas an almost pizzalike flavor when mixed with meaty portobellos and cheese. The oven-dried tomatoes are great on their own, and can be used on salads to give them an intense summery flavor. They take a few unattended hours to prepare, but can be made a day or two in advance. For a delightful alternative, try substituting grilled shrimp and peppers for the tomatoes and mushrooms.

9 Roma tomatoes, cored and halved

$^3/_4$ cup Herb Marinade for Grilled Vegetables (page 52)

$^1/_4$ cup olive oil

4 large portobello mushrooms

6 to 8 large cloves garlic, dry-roasted and coarsely chopped (see page 116)

Salt and pepper to taste

Four 12-inch flour tortillas

5 cups (20 ounces) grated Monterey jack or Muenster cheese

12 large fresh basil leaves

4 tablespoons butter at room temperature

$^1/_2$ cup Ancho Crema (page 101), optional

$^1/_3$ cup diagonally cut scallion rings, green part only

Preheat the oven to 250°. Dip the tomatoes in the well-stirred marinade and put them, cut-side up, on a wire rack or grill screen that has been placed on a baking sheet. Put the pan in the oven for 2 to 3 hours, or until the tomatoes are wrinkled but still fairly moist. Turn off the oven and leave the tomatoes inside for 6 to 8 hours, or until firm but flexible. Cut 3 to 4 tomato pieces into strips for garnishing the finished quesadillas and set aside.

In a large sauté pan or skillet on medium-high heat, heat the olive oil and sauté the mushrooms, stirring gently and occasionally, for 5 to 7 minutes, or until golden brown. Add the chopped garlic and cook for another 30 seconds. Season with salt and pepper to taste and turn them out into a shallow pan to cool.

To assemble the quesadillas, heat a griddle, large sauté pan, or large skillet over medium heat and cook 2 tortillas, one at a time, for 5 to 10 seconds on each side to make them pliable. Lay the tortillas out on a work surface. Sprinkle half of each tortilla with about $^1/_3$ cup of the cheese, leaving a $^1/_2$-inch margin at the outer edge. Distribute the dried tomato halves over the cheese. Sprinkle about $^1/_3$ cup of the cheese over the tomatoes and layer the mushrooms and garlic over the top. Arrange 3 basil leaves over the mushrooms and top with the remaining cheese. Fold the uncovered half of each tortilla over the filling and press it gently. Repeat to fill and fold the remaining tortillas. The quesadillas may be prepared to this point up to 12 hours in advance, covered, and refrigerated.

If the quesadillas have been refrigerated, let them sit at room temperature for 5 minutes before cooking them. To prevent the basil leaves from turning black, cook the quesadillas as close to serving time as possible. Preheat oven to 250°. Brush the tops of the quesadillas with half of the butter and place them buttered side down on the griddle or in the skillet. Reduce the heat to medium and cook for 2 or 3 minutes, or until crisp and golden brown. Brush the tops of the quesadillas with the remaining butter. Using a spatula, turn them carefully and cook on the other side for 2 or 3 minutes. It may be necessary to cook the quesadillas in 2 batches. If so, hold the cooked ones on a wire rack or baking sheet in the warm oven while cooking the remainder. When ready to serve, cut the quesadillas into the desired number of wedges and arrange them on 4 warm serving plates.

Streak the finished quesadillas with Ancho Crema, if desired. Divide the reserved tomato strips over the quesadillas and sprinkle the scallions over to garnish. Serve at once.

Barbecued Beef Quesadillas presented as hors d'oeuvres (top left) and as a light entrée (bottom)

cremas and streakers

One of the most enjoyable aspects of cooking today's southwestern food is decorating plates and food with squirt bottles. It is fun to watch culinarians emulate Jackson Pollock as they squiggle and splatter and zigzag their way to presentation glory. Most southwestern cooks have a strong aversion to boring presentations and stark white plates, and ancho, black bean, or avocado streakers can decorate the rims of bowls and plates, and add a touch of whimsy to spicy dishes.

Mexican crema, or *crema espesa*, is rich unpasteurized cream that has thickened naturally by setting at room temperature, much like crème fraîche. Drizzled over enchiladas, quesadillas, and other spicy dishes, its tang and richness provides a welcome counterpoint to hot foods. Squeeze bottles are a great way to add crema in thin delicate ribbons that don't pour on the fat and calories. Nonfat "streakers" can be made with different-colored bean purées that have been thinned with water or stock.

1. Make the crema according to your chosen recipe. It may be necessary to thin the finished product with a few drops of buttermilk or milk to achieve the desired consistency. For flavored cremas such as ancho or mango, use the thickest possible crema or sour

cream, because it will thin from being stirred and from the addition of flavoring agents. Using either a paper cone or a funnel, fill squeeze bottles with the finished crema. The bottles can be filled up to 1 day in advance, the tips wrapped with plastic wrap, and refrigerated. Let them sit at room temperature for 5 minutes before using.

2. Make extra crema and practice designs and techniques on plates or a cutting board. The tips of the bottles can be trimmed with a sharp knife to make either thin or thick ribbons to your liking. Remember that when it comes to design, the only rule is that there are no rules. Add cremas and streakers just before serving, as they will dry and/or crack when exposed to the air for extended periods of time, and they will bleed into sauces after a few minutes.

what not to do

1. **Don't overdo it. The charm of streakers is that they add snippets of flavor and a colorful little punch to the dishes. Apply too much over sauces and finished dishes, and you can mask the hard work that went into the dish itself. Always think in terms of complementary flavors when choosing a crema or streaker, remembering that it is taste that matters first and foremost.**

2. **When garnishing the rims of plates and bowls, decorate just the area of the dish that will be served *away* from the guests. More than one restaurant has had to pay dry-cleaning bills for patrons who dragged their sleeves through these masterpieces.**

crema

makes about 1 cup

In Mexican homes and markets, thick unpasteurized cream is left to sit in the warm air, where the natural bacteria go to work to create a rich, tangy cream that adds a contrast to chile-infused dishes. Of course, unpasteurized cream has long been taboo in the United States, and many of us have never tasted real crema or crème fraîche. This recipe comes close, making a tangy and luscious crema with scant effort.

1 cup heavy cream
1 tablespoon buttermilk

Whisk the cream and buttermilk together in a small bowl. Cover the bowl with a towel and put it in a warm place such as a gas oven or near a water heater. The crema should thicken in 8 to 10 hours. Cover and refrigerate for 1 hour or until needed. When chilled, the crema may need to be thinned with a few drops of buttermilk to achieve a proper consistency for streaking. Pour it through a funnel into a squeeze bottle and refriger-

ate until needed. Wrap the tip of the bottle with plastic wrap to prevent off flavors from creeping in. Before using the crema, let it sit at room temperature for 5 minutes or so, then hold your finger over the tip and give the bottle a good shake. The crema will keep for up to 1 week in the refrigerator.

VARIATION: An even simpler crema can be made by whisking 2 tablespoons of buttermilk into 1 cup of sour cream.

ancho crema

makes 1 cup

Although cremas and other streakers can add colorful flourishes to food and plate rims, that whimsy can quickly turn to frustration when the tip of the squeeze bottle clogs. Make sure that the ancho purée is well strained before making this crema.

$^3/_4$ cup Crema or sour cream
2 tablespoons Ancho Purée (see page 26)
$^1/_4$ teaspoon salt or to taste
Juice of $^1/_2$ lime

Combine all the ingredients in a small bowl and whisk well to blend. Taste and adjust the seasoning, Pour the crema through a paper cone or funnel into a squeeze bottle. If you are not using it right away, wrap the tip of the bottle with plastic wrap and refrigerate for up to 2 days. Let the crema sit at room temperature for about 5 minutes, then cover the top of the bottle with your finger and give the bottle a good shake before using.

avocado crema

makes 1 1/4 cups

This crema brings the flavor and color of avocado to dishes without the worry about finding the fickle fruit when it is perfectly ripe. The light acidity of the sour cream and the zing of the lime juice will maintain the color of the crema for up to 3 days. For color and flavor variation, substitute mango or papaya for the avocado.

1 ripe avocado, peeled, pitted, and chopped
1/4 cup buttermilk
Juice of 1 lime
3/4 cup Crema (page 101) or sour cream
1/2 teaspoon salt or to taste

Put the avocado in a blender with the buttermilk and lime juice. Purée until quite smooth, adding some of the sour cream if necessary to create a smooth purée. Scrape the avocado purée into a bowl, add the sour cream, and whisk well to blend. Stir in the salt. Pour the crema through a paper cone or funnel into a squeeze bottle. If you are not using the crema right away, wrap the tip of the bottle with plastic wrap and refrigerate for up to 3 days.

Let the crema sit at room temperature for about 5 minutes before using, then place your finger over the tip, and give the bottle a quick shake before using.

nonfat black bean streaker

makes 1 1/2 cups

This is a fine way to add a touch of drama to the rims of plates and bowls and to provide a flavor contrast to light meats and sauces.

1 cup drained warm cooked black beans (see page 117)
3/4 cup bean broth or water, warmed
2 teaspoons Chipotles en Adobe Purée (page 26)
3/4 teaspoon salt

Put the ingredients in a blender and purée until very smooth. Taste and adjust the seasoning. Force the purée through a fine-meshed sieve with the back of a large spoon. Pour the purée through a funnel or paper cone into a squeeze bottle. If you are not using it right away, cover the top with plastic wrap and refrigerate for up to 3 days. Let the purée sit at room temperature for about 5 minutes before using.

Oven-dried Tomato, Mushroom, and Roasted Garlic Quesadilla finished with Ancho Crema and Crema (top left), Fresh Corn Tamales served on Cactus Escabeche with Roasted Corn and Roma Tomatos garnished with Nonfat Black Bean Streaker (middle right), Chorizo and Potato Enchiladas in Blue Corn Tortillas streaked with Crema (bottom)

flans

In many Mexican restaurants in the United States, the dessert course offers two options: flan, or no flan. Spanish nuns introduced prepared sweets to this continent, making candies and cookies to sell for the benefit of their orders. Flan originated in Spain as a way to utilize the egg yolks left over from sherry production, in which egg whites were used to clarify the wine before it was poured into oak barrels for aging. Though the name changed, this dish is found in various forms throughout Europe and is one of the most popular desserts in America, where it goes by the name, créme caramel.

The light, smooth, and benign texture of flan is welcome to a palate that has been overwhelmed by a spicy or heavy meal. Flan can be made in individual molds for elegant presentations and easy portioning, or in a large cake pan or ring and served sliced when well chilled. Its delicate flavor makes it a prime candidate for variation. Ginger, spices, liqueurs, low-acid fruits, nuts, and chocolate can all lend their character in infinite combinations. The beauty of flan is that it needs almost no embellishment to be made complete. The caramel softens to make a sauce that swirls around the finished dessert, and it needs little if anything else to complement.

1. Preheat the oven to 300°. Butter or spray the mold or molds for your flan and put them aside. Measure the sugar and lemon juice for the caramel into a heavy saucepan and stir it over medium heat for 1 to 2 minutes, or until the sugar melts.

2. Cook the sugar for 6 to 8 minutes, or until it has reached a golden brown color, brushing the sides of the pot occasionally with a pastry brush that has been dipped into water to prevent the formation of crystals. Caramel will continue to

cook after it is removed from heat if it is not "shocked" by setting the saucepan in a bowl of ice. Be careful not to get ice or water inside the pan, as a boil-over could result. If the caramel becomes too thick or hardens, warm it over very low heat until it is soft again. Spoon the cooled caramel into the mold or molds.

3. If infusing milk, bring it to a strong simmer and add any spices or flavorings called for in the recipe. Allow the liquids to steep for 20 minutes off heat or as directed in the recipe. Strain if necessary. Let the milk cool to room temperature before proceeding. (Many recipes for Mexican flan call for simmering the milk to reduce the volume by as much as half, a

lighter version using unreduced whole milk is preferred by most Americans.) Gradually whisk the sugar into the yolks to avoid "burning" the yolks, causing lumps. Pour in the milk in a steady stream and whisk until all the ingredients are blended. Strain the custard through a fine-meshed sieve and pour it into the mold or molds.

4. Place the mold(s) in a large baking pan. Add water to $^1/_3$ to $^1/_2$ of the way up the sides of the mold(s). Cook for 20 to 30

minutes, or until just set. Carefully remove the mold(s) from the water bath. Once the flans have cooled to room temperature, cover and refrigerate for at least 4 hours, and preferably overnight, before attempting to unmold. When ready to serve, loosen the flan from the edges of the mold with your fingertips or a sharp knife pressed firmly against the edges of the pan. Unmold individual flans directly onto a serving plate. To unmold a large flan, put the serving plate on top of the mold and hold both mold and plate in the center with each hand while inverting the mold and plate.

what not to do

1. **Don't cook the flan at too high a temperature. Some recipes call for oven settings as high as 400°. At such temperatures, the custard takes on a pocked texture and will be watery in consistency.**

2. **Take great caution to avoid caramel burns, which are extremely painful. Do not touch or taste the caramel as it cooks, and take care not to add any liquid to the caramel until it has cooled to slightly warmer than room temperature.**

orange and canela flan

makes 6 individual flans

This is a southwestern variation on the vanilla-infused créme caramels of our youth. Orange zest and canela seem to be an inevitable flavor combination for the velvety smooth custard.

FOR THE CARAMEL

1 tablespoon water

$^1/_2$ cup sugar

FOR THE CUSTARD

2 cups milk

Small pinch of salt

Three 2-inch sticks canela, or 1 $^1/_2$ sticks cinnamon

Peel of 1 orange, left as whole as possible with the white pith removed

3 eggs

2 egg yolks

6 tablespoons sugar

Preheat the oven to 300°. Lightly butter six 4-ounce ramekins or custard cups. To make the caramel, stir together the water and sugar in a heavy pot over medium-high heat. Using a pastry brush dipped in water, brush the sides of the pot just above the sugar every minute or so to prevent crystals from forming. Cook the sugar until a rich dark color is achieved. Since the caramel will continue to cook once it has been removed

from the heat, it should be "shocked" to prevent it from becoming too dark and bitter. This is best done by setting the pot into a bowl of ice. Be very careful not to get ice or water inside the pot, as a boil-over could result. Spoon the cooled caramel into the mold or molds. If the caramel becomes too thick or sets up completely, warm it over very low heat until it is pliable again. Pour about 2 teaspoons caramel into each mold and tilt them from side to side to coat the bottom. Reserve the remaining caramel for garnish.

For the custard, combine the milk, salt, and canela in a medium saucepan. Bring the milk to a strong simmer over medium-high heat, stir in the orange peel, and remove from the heat. Let the milk cool for 30 minutes. Combine the eggs and egg yolks in a medium bowl and whisk in the sugar until the mixture is blended but not foamy. Strain the milk into the eggs and sugar and whisk until blended. Pour the custard into the prepared molds. Place the molds in a baking pan and place in the oven. Add water to $^1/_3$ to $^1/_2$ of the way up the sides of the molds. Bake the flans for 45 minutes to 1 hour, or until set. Remove the flans carefully from the water bath and allow them to cool to room temperature. Cover tightly and refrigerate them at least 4 hours or up to overnight.

When ready to serve, loosen the flans from the edges of the mold with your fingertips or a sharp knife pressed firmly against the edges of the pan. Unmold individual flans directly onto their serving plates. If making one large flan, put the serving plate on top of the mold and invert them both in tandem. Lift the mold off carefully. If desired, rewarm the remaining caramel with a few drops of water and drizzle around the flans.

Cajeta Flan (top), Orange and Canela Flan (bottom)

cajeta flan

makes 6 individual flans

A cajeta *was originally a little wooden box made to hold sweets, but the name was eventually given to a sweet paste of nuts, fruit, or milk. Goat's milk cajeta is made by flavoring goat's milk with canela, then cooking it thickens and takes on a caramel quality. In this recipe, the cajeta is used as a base for flan. The cajeta is also wonderful as an ice cream topping or as a spread for shortcakes. Although the baking soda will encourage the sugar to caramelize as the cajeta cooks, you may wish to brown the sugar separately before adding it to achieve an even richer color and flavor. But allow the caramel to cool almost to room temperature before adding it, as a dangerous boil-over might occur.*

FOR THE CAJETA

4 cups goat's milk

Two 2-inch sticks canela, or 1 stick cinnamon

1 cup sugar

$^1/_2$ teaspoon baking soda

$^1/_2$ teaspoon water

FOR THE CARAMEL

1 tablespoon water

$^1/_2$ cup sugar

Juice of $^1/_2$ lemon

Softened butter for lightly brushing the molds

FOR THE CUSTARD

3 eggs

3 egg yolks

3 tablespoons sugar

1 $^1/_4$ cups milk

Combine the goat's milk and canela or cinnamon in a medium-sized saucepan. Over medium-high heat, bring milk mixture to a simmer, stirring often to prevent it from boiling over. If desired, caramelize the sugar in the same manner as discussed below and add it to the goat's milk after it has cooled. Otherwise add the sugar to the goat's milk at the beginning. (If you are caramelizing all the sugar, you may make it all at once, using $^2/_3$ for the cajeta and reserving the remainder for lining the molds and drizzling around the plates.) Combine the baking soda with the water and stir this mixture into the milk. Simmer the cajeta until it has reduced to about $^3/_4$ cup, about 20 minutes. Strain and refrigerate for up to one week, tightly covered.

To make the caramel, lightly butter six 4-ounce ramekins or custard cups. Stir together the water, lemon juice, and sugar in a heavy pot over medium-high heat. Using a pastry brush dipped in water, brush the sides of the pot just above the sugar every minute or so to prevent crystals from forming. Cook the sugar until a rich dark color is achieved. Since the caramel will continue to cook once it has been removed from the heat, it should be "shocked" to prevent it from becoming too dark and bitter. This is best done by setting the pot into a bowl of ice. Be very careful not to get ice or water inside the pot, as a boil-over could result. Spoon the cooled caramel into the prepared molds. If the caramel becomes too thick or sets up completely, warm it over very low heat until it is pliable again. Pour 2 teaspoons of caramel into each mold and turn the molds to evenly coat the bottom. If desired, reserve the remaining caramel to pour around the finished desserts, thinned with a few drops of warm water.

To finish the flan, preheat the oven to 300°. Warm the cajeta slightly in the microwave or allow it to come to room termperature. Put the eggs and egg yolks in a medium bowl and whisk in the 3 tablespoons of sugar until it is dissolved but the mixture is not foamy. Whisk in the cajeta and then the milk, and stir until well blended. Pour the custard into the prepared molds and place them in a water bath. Place the flans into a preheated oven and bake for 20 to 30 minutes, or until firm. Carefully remove the flans from the water bath and chill, tightly covered, for 4 hours to overnight before serving.

When ready to serve, loosen the flans from the edges of the mold with your fingertips or a sharp knife pressed firmly against the edges of the pan. Unmold individual flans directly onto their serving plates. If making one large flan, put the serving plate on top of the mold and invert them in tandem. Lift the mold off carefully. Drizzle the reserved caramel around, if desired, and serve at once.

chocolate and banana flan

makes 6 individual flans

If ever two foods were meant to be paired together, they are chocolate and bananas, and this dessert is absolutely delicious. Milk chocolate provides a more delicate and superior flavor, but chocolate-lovers may prefer the more chocolatey look and taste created by using semisweet chocolate and cocoa. Using banana peels rather than banana to flavor the custard helps to maintain the gentle texture of the finished dessert.

FOR THE CARAMEL

Softened butter for lightly brushing the molds

1 tablespoon water

$^1/_2$ cup sugar

Juice of $^1/_2$ lemon

FOR THE CUSTARD

2 cups milk

Peels from 2 ripe bananas

1 small pinch of salt

3 eggs

3 egg yolks

5 tablespoons sugar

5 ounces milk chocolate, chopped, or
**   3 ounces semisweet chocolate, chopped, and**
**   1 tablespoon cocoa**

To make the caramel, lightly butter six 4-ounce ramekins or custard cups. Stir together the water, lemon juice, and sugar in a heavy pot over medium-high heat. Using a pastry brush dipped in water, brush the sides of the pot just above the sugar every minute or so to prevent crystals from forming. Cook the sugar until a rich dark color is achieved. Since the caramel will continue to cook once it has been removed from the heat, it should be "shocked" to prevent it from becoming too dark and bitter. This is best done by setting the pot into a bowl of ice. Be very careful not to get ice or water inside the pot, as a boil-over could result. Spoon the cooled caramel into the prepared molds. If the caramel becomes too thick or sets up completely, warm it over very low heat until it is pliable again. Pour 2 teaspoons of caramel into each mold and turn the molds to evenly coat the bottom. If desired, reserve the remaining caramel to pour around the finished desserts, warmed, thinned with a few drops of water, and drizzled around.

For the custard, combine the milk, banana peels, and salt in a medium saucepan. Bring the milk to a strong simmer and turn off the heat. Let the milk cool for at least 30 minutes.

Combine the eggs and egg yolks in a medium bowl and whisk in the 5 tablespoons of sugar until the mixture is blended but not foamy. Melt the chocolate in a bowl over simmering water until it is just smooth. Do not overheat it. Strain the milk through a fine sieve into the chocolate, pressing the banana peels with the back of a large spoon to extract all of the milk. Discard the peels. Whisk the milk into the egg mixture to blend well. Pour the custard into the prepared molds and place them in a water bath. Place the flans into a preheated oven and bake for 20 to 30 minutes or until firm. Carefully remove the flans from the water bath and chill for 4 hours to overnight before serving.

When ready to serve, loosen the flans from the edges of the mold with your fingertips or a sharp knife pressed firmly against the edges of the pan. Unmold individual flans directly onto their serving plates. If you are making one large flan, put the serving plate on top of the mold and invert them in tandem. Lift the mold off carefully. Drizzle the reserved caramel around, if desired, and serve at once.

cobblers and crumbles

The cobbler is a classic western dessert. In their home on the frontier, pioneer children collected buckets of wild berries. Mom put them in a Dutch oven with a sprinkling of precious sugar and topped them with her best drop biscuit dough. The covered vessel was placed over the coals of the evening fire, and the biscuit topping baked as the berries oozed their dark nectar, which mingled with the dense crust. Too bad they couldn't make ice cream on the prairie.

There are two different theories about the word *cobbler*. According to the first, the dessert was so named because the mounds of dough resemble a cobblestone street when the dish is baked. The second theory is that the name comes from the verb "to cobble," which means both to mend or patch coarsely—possibly a description of the uneven topping—or to whip something up in a hurry, an apt description of the speed with which cobblers are made.

Crumbles and crisps are similar to cobblers in that they are simple to prepare and are at their best when made with the freshest fruits of the season. The topping consists of a mixture of flour, oats, or another grain, sugars, and usually nuts and spices with butter cut in.

When making cobblers or crumbles from juicy or frozen fruits, mix about $^1/_2$ teaspoon of cornstarch or flour per cup of fruit with the sugar for the filling. This will thicken the juices as the cobbler cooks, and will help to keep the topping from becoming gooey as it bakes. The amount of thickener given here should be used only as a guideline, however, as the moisture content of fruit varies.

to make cobblers

1. Make the topping according to the chosen recipe. Sprinkle the sugar and any other flavorings over the fruit and toss or stir just enough to coat them evenly.

2. Butter an appropriate dish and pour in the fruit filling. Either drop dollops of the topping over the fruit or, if using a pourable topping, spoon it on and spread it with a spatula. Bake, cool, and serve the cobbler as instructed in the recipe.

to make crumbles

Prepare the filling according to the recipe and place it in a buttered dish. Cut the cold butter for the topping into 1-inch cubes. Combine all the dry ingredients in a bowl, stir to blend, and add the cold butter. Using either a pastry cutter or your fingers, mix the ingredients together, breaking the butter down into small bits about the size of peanuts. Do not over-mix. The topping should consist of irregularly sized pieces. Sprinkle the topping over the fruit filling in an even layer and bake according to the chosen recipe.

what not to do

1. Don't use soupy fillings, which will yield a soggy topping and runny filling. Denser fruits such as plums should be tossed in sugar and drained in a strainer for 30 minutes or so to remove excess liquid, and if you must use thawed frozen fruits, be sure to drain them well before proceeding.

2. Make sure that the topping is done. Cobblers, especially, can be misleading, and it can be embarrassing to serve one only to discover that a liquid and floury mass is lurking just beneath the majestic crust. If you are using a new recipe, test for doneness. A knife or wooden skewer inserted in the topping should come out clean.

champagne and peach cobbler with dried cherries

makes one medium cobbler; serves 6

If you couldn't quite finish off that bottle of bubbly last night, champagne adds a welcome and indulgent touch to this cobbler. Cinnamon, champagne, and peaches are another ageless flavor combination, and tart cherries provide a welcome counterpoint. If you are cooking for a group of cobbler purists, you can always leave out the champagne and cherries and replace them with an extra cup of peaches.

$^3/_4$ **cup tart dried cherries**

6 fresh medium-sized peaches, peeled, pitted, and sliced

$^1/_2$ **cup sugar**

1 tablespoon ground canela, or 1$^1/_2$ teaspoons ground cinnamon

Juice of 2 limes

$^1/_2$ **cup champagne or dry white wine**

FOR THE TOPPING

1$^1/_2$ cups all-purpose flour

2 teaspoons baking powder

$^1/_4$ **teaspoon salt**

3 tablespoons sugar

$^1/_2$ **teaspoon ground ginger**

$^1/_2$ **teaspoon ground canela, or $^1/_4$ teaspoon ground cinnamon**

6 tablespoons cold butter, cut into 1-inch cubes

$^3/_4$ **cup milk**

1 tablespoon cornstarch

$^1/_2$ **cup sugar plus 1$^1/_2$ tablespoons sugar for sprinkling (optional)**

3 tablespoons butter, melted

$^1/_3$ **teaspoon ground cinnamon for sprinkling (optional)**

Soak the cherries in warm water to cover for 30 minutes. Drain them well and combine them in a large bowl with the peaches, $^1/_2$ cup of the sugar, the canela, and lime juice. Pour the champagne over and stir just to mix. Let sit for 1 hour at room temperature.

Preheat the oven to 375°. For the topping, stir the flour, baking powder, salt, 3 tablespoons of sugar, ginger, and canela in a large bowl. Cut in the cold butter with a pastry cutter or your fingers until the pieces are the size of peas. Pour in the milk and stir just until a soft dough is formed. Do not overmix.

Stir the cornstarch into the $^1/_2$ cup sugar. Drain the fruit of all liquid except a light coating. Toss the peaches and cherries in the cornstarch and sugar mixture and pour them into the baking dish. Drizzle the melted butter over the fruit. Drop the topping on the fruit in heaping spoonfuls, covering most of the surface of the cobbler. Leave $^1/_2$-inch gaps between the spoonfuls of topping. If desired, combine the 1$^1/_2$ tablespoons sugar with the cinnamon and sprinkle it over the cobbler. Bake for 40 to 45 minutes or until the topping is a golden color, the fruit begins to bubble, and a knife or wooden skewer inserted in the dough comes out clean. Let cobbler cool slightly before serving.

Blackberry and Three-Citrus Cobbler (top right), Champagne and Peach Cobbler with Dried Cherries (top left), Blueberry, Orange, and Plum Crumble with ice cream (bottom)

blackberry and three-citrus cobbler

makes 1 medium cobbler; serves 6

Washington, D.C.–area pastry chef and gardener par excellence Dan Michel appropriated this recipe from his amateur-chef father-in-law Tom Allen. The topping is a spreadable one that works well with most soft fruits and berries. For a tropical-flavored filling, try substituting bananas for half of the blackberries called for below.

FOR THE FILLING

4 cups fresh blackberries

1 teaspoon minced or grated orange zest

$^1/_2$ teaspoon minced or grated lemon zest

$^1/_2$ teaspoon minced or grated lime zest

1 tablespoon cornstarch

$^1/_2$ cup sugar

FOR THE TOPPING

1 cup all-purpose flour

1 cup sugar

1 teaspoon baking powder

1 teaspoon ground canela, or $^1/_2$ teaspoon ground cinnamon

$^1/_4$ teaspoon ground mace

$^1/_4$ teaspoon salt

1 cup milk

$^1/_2$ teaspoon vanilla extract

$^1/_2$ cup (1 stick) butter, melted

For the filling, combine the berries and zests in a medium bowl and stir gently. Mix the cornstarch and sugar together in a small bowl. Add this mixture to the fruit and toss to coat it. Let the fruit sit for 30 minutes to 1 hour.

Preheat the oven to 375°. For the topping, stir the flour, sugar, baking powder, canela, mace, and salt together in a medium bowl. Mix the milk and vanilla together and stir it into the dry ingredients in a steady stream. Fold in the melted butter.

Turn the filling into a 12-inch baking dish. Pour the topping over and spread it with a rubber spatula to cover the fruit. Bake the cobbler for 30 to 45 minutes, or until the fruit bubbles, the topping is golden, and a toothpick inserted in the topping comes out clean. Let the cobbler cool slightly before serving.

blueberry, orange, and plum crumble

makes 1 large crumble; serves 6 to 8

The cultivating of blueberries began in New Jersey in the summer of 1920. The boggy soils of the Northeastern states were considered to be worthless for agriculture until several previously wild "bilberry" cultivars were introduced. Quite a few summers have passed since then, but the flavors of this simple dessert remain timeless. For an extra taste of heaven, serve this crumble with a premium vanilla ice cream.

FOR THE FILLING

4 ripe plums, pitted and diced

6 tablespoons sugar

2 teaspoons cornstarch

4 teaspoons ground canela, or 2 teaspoons ground cinnamon

4 oranges, peeled and cut into sections

2 cups fresh blueberries

FOR THE TOPPING

1 cup old-fashioned rolled oats

$^1/_2$ cup all-purpose flour

$^1/_2$ cup packed brown sugar

1 tablespoon ground canela, or 1 $^1/_2$ teaspoons ground cinnamon

$^1/_4$ teaspoon ground nutmeg

$^1/_4$ cup hazelnuts, toasted, skinned, and chopped (see page 117)

Pinch of salt

6 tablespoons cold butter

Minced zest of $^1/_2$ orange

For the filling, put the plums in a medium bowl, add 3 tablespoons of the sugar, and toss to coat the plums. Put the mixture in a sieve and drain for 30 minutes to 1 hour. Stir the cornstarch and canela into the remaining 5 tablespoons sugar, add it to the plums, oranges, and blueberries and toss to coat it, and pour the filling into a 12-inch baking dish. To make the topping, put all the dry ingredients except the orange zest into a large mixing bowl and stir well. Cut the chilled butter into 1-inch cubes and toss into the dry ingredients along with the orange zest. Using either a pastry cutter or your fingers, work the butter into the dry ingredients until peanut-sized pieces are formed. The mixture will be loose and fairly dry. The crumble topping may be made in advance, covered, and refrigerated for up to 5 days.

To bake, preheat the oven to 375°. Sprinkle the crumble topping over the filling and bake the crumble for 30 to 40 minutes, or until the topping browns and the fruit bubbles. Let cool slightly before serving.

a little more

dry-roasting vegetables

Someone should create a new synonym for the word earthy, for there is no other way to describe the intense rustic dimension that the following simple methods bring to the dishes of the southwestern kitchen. Dry-roasting, or roasting in a dry pan, allows vegetables to be prepared without added oils or fats, and they take on a deep nutty character that evokes the spirit of the great outdoors. Garlic that has been broken down into individual cloves and roasted unpeeled takes on a straw-like and hazelnut depth and a sweetness that richly rewards the modicum of effort and attention required to produce it. Although tomatillos are usually used raw or fire-roasted as shown on pages 18–19, some recipes call for them to be dry-roasted to develop a deeper, mellower, and almost herblike flavor.

dry-roasting tomatillos and garlic

To dry-roast denser vegetables such as tomatillos and garlic, put them on a dry skillet over low to medium heat. Since you are not trying to sear the foods, it is not necessary to preheat the pan. Tomatillos and garlic will take about 20 to 30 minutes to roast through, but will not require constant attention as long as the heat remains low. Check on them every 5 minutes or so and turn them as needed to achieve an evenly colored vegetable that is soft to the touch. Be sure not to overcrowd the pan, so that the food will have room to cook evenly. The temptation will be strong to start roasting the tomatillos and garlic on the stove and then transfer them to the oven to finish them. This method will cook them through just fine, but it will not provide them with the nuttiness that brings so much character to the finished products. Direct contact with the heat source is vital.

dry-roasting corn kernels and mushrooms

For smaller, quick-cooking items such as corn kernels and quartered mushrooms, high heat and a hot pan are necessary to cook and brown the food quickly. Heat the sauté pan or seasoned cast-iron skillet well and add the food to be roasted. If you are cooking late-season corn or particularly dry mushrooms, it may be necessary to add a drop or two of oil to prevent scorching. Add just enough food to cover the bottom of the skillet. Corn should be no more than 2 or 3 kernels deep. Let the food sizzle and brown around the edges before turning it. Ideally, foods should be turned no more than 3 or 4 times to allow them to brown and roast. Because of their high sugar content, corn kernels will become deep brown, almost black, over about half of their surface. This caramelization adds a wonderful woodsiness to sauces, salsas, and stuffings.

toasting seeds, herbs, and spices

To toast pepitas, place them, about 2 seeds deep, in a shallow sauté pan or skillet. Place the pan over medium heat and let it sit until the seeds begin to pop and toast. Stir the seeds occasionally for 5 to 8 minutes, or until the popping stops and the seeds have taken on a toasted and olive cast.

Spices and dried herbs have been toasted for almost as long as people have been drying them for storage. But the way that they mingle with chiles and the slow-cooked flavors of the Southwest makes the practice seem almost original to this cuisine. Cumin, coriander, and dried herbs such as Mexican oregano awaken from their dormancy and lend a romantic and natural perfume to the kitchen as well as to the foods being prepared. Place a shallow layer of herbs or spices in a dry sauté pan over medium to high heat. As the spices darken around the edges, stir or flip them. When they have released their perfume and darken slightly, they are done, usually in less than 1 minute. Herbs and spices will burn quickly if left unattended, so watch them carefully.

cooking beans

It is difficult to overstate the importance of the humble bean in southwestern, Mexican, and Native American cooking. As part of the "holy trinity" that also included corn and squashes, they were vital to the sustenance of most Native American cultures. Many a drought and harsh winter were survived on a store of dried beans that had been simmered with a few shreds of jerky and dried wild herbs for flavor. Anxious pioneers heading west often had little else to sustain them as they passed over treacherous terrain and barren deserts en route to an uncertain new home. Prospectors, making desperate

passage to stake their claim, often ignored the bounties of nature altogether and dined only on beans and salt pork, so as not to waste precious travel time hunting fresh meat or gathering wild greens.

Today, beans can provide an elegant dimension to meals. Antique or heirloom varieties such as Jacob's Cattle and Steuben Yelloweyes are making a strong comeback. Originally grown by the Algonquin Indians, Yelloweyes were passed on to the early settlers to become the original Boston baked beans. Colorful and variegated beans eventually fell out of favor because their variegated colors bled together when they were canned. But now, as we return to a more holistic diet with a reverence for history and nature, varieties such as Chestnut Lima and others that very nearly became extinct are increasingly easier to find.

Part of the challenge of a properly cooked bean may lie with the proliferation of these heirloom and antique varieties. These beans are usually much fresher and less dry than commodity beans such as black turtles and kidney beans, which may be held by the farmer for as long as two years while he waits for favorable pricing. Hence, soaking and cooking times vary much more than in the past.

Before cooking dried beans, spread them out onto a flat contained surface such as a sided baking sheet and pick through them to remove any small stones, debris, and broken and discolored beans. Next, place the beans in a bowl or the pot in which they will be cooked, and pour boiling water or very hot water over them. For variegated beans, use plenty of water. This will leach out some of the color and prevent the hues from mingling as the beans cook.

Let the beans soak for 1 hour, then pour off the liquid and replace it with fresh cool water. Use at least 3 times more water than beans. Large volumes of water will keep the carbohydrates from developing into a starchy film as the beans cook, resulting in a cooked bean with a firmer, less mushy texture. Fresh herbs, garlic, and other spices that will need to be removed later should be tied into a bundle or wrapped in a cheesecloth and tied into a sachet.

Cook beans for 45 to 90 minutes, or until they are tender but firm and not mealy. If the beans will be puréed, cook them until they are quite tender. Never salt beans until the last few moments of cooking. Salt causes the skins to toughen and makes it harder for the beans to take on moisture and absorb the flavor of the spices.

brines and marinades

One of the best and easiest ways to impart flavors to food is with a well-chosen brine or marinade. Although they are sometimes used to tame the wildness of strong game, brines and marinades primarily enhance and complement the natural flavors of food. Since the sauces of the Southwest are so assertive and robust, mild meats such as chicken, pork, and quail, as well as delicate fish such as halibut and grouper, often need to be marinated so that they can maintain their true character without being overwhelmed.

Food is usually submerged in brines to cure or "cook" it prior to cold or hot smoking or grilling. The brines are flavored with spices and herbs and, in the case of pork and red meats, very small quantities of nitrates. Much has been written about the use of sodium nitrate, or "pink salt," and its effects on our health. The truth is that the small quantity used in cured and smoked meats is not sufficient to pose a great risk to even the most voracious consumer. Smoking causes pink and red meats to oxidize and turn gray. Without the addition of a little pink salt, most meats from the smokehouse would be an unappetizing gray color, and thus would be avoided by diners in droves. Now that the disclaimer is out of the way, it can be said that brines are terrific for adding flavor and improving the texture of foods.

Although many cooks and chefs insist that marinating actually tenderizes meat, they in fact do little in that regard. They can, over time, soften meat slightly, but this change occurs only on the surface. Unless the marinade contains pineapple, figs, or papaya, all of which are used in many modern meat tenderizers (and can turn most meats to mush if not used carefully), marinades are basically flavoring agents. But what marvelous agents they can be. Meat, fish, and vegetables cooked on the grill should be mandated by law to spend at least a little time in a tart herb-infused bath, which will add moisture and layers of flavor. If only for the olfactory enjoyment of the person tending the fire, marinades should become a standard part of your repertoire.

orange-chipotle marinade

makes about 1 ¹/₄ cups

Smoked jalapeño and orange is a combination of flavors that always works. This marinade is good for seafood, pork, and poultry, and may be used to bake a ceviche-style filling for a chilled relleno (see page 66). The marinade can be reduced further and strained to make a sauce or glaze that is loaded with flavor.

4 cups fresh orange juice

¹/₂ tablespoon chopped Chipotles en Adobo (page 25) or to taste

1 teaspoon adobo sauce

3 large cloves garlic, dry-roasted (see page 116)

2 tablespoons coarsely chopped fresh basil

2 teaspoons olive oil

¹/₂ teaspoon salt or to taste

1 tablespoon honey

Juice of 1 lime

3 tablespoons balsamic vinegar

Pour the orange juice into a medium saucepan and bring it to a boil. Reduce the heat to a strong simmer and cook to reduce the liquid to about 1 cup, about 30 minutes. Let cool. Stir in all the remaining ingredients. Taste and adjust the seasoning.

Pour the cool marinade over meat, poultry, or seafood in a shallow nonreactive pan, cover, and refrigerate. Chicken and cuts of pork should marinate for 2 to 4 hours. Fish and shellfish should marinate for 1 to 2 hours before being grilled or sautéed.

scallion and cilantro marinade

makes about 1 cup

Swordfish, chicken, and other light meats that spend some time in this marinade take on a vibrant green hue as well as a zesty, fresh flavor. From both an appearance and a flavor viewpoint, this is a good marinade for meats that are served with red pipiáns and rich dark moles. It also pairs well with tomato and tropical fruit salsas.

¹/₂ cup scallions, green part only, cut into rings

¹/₂ cup packed fresh cilantro leaves

7 cloves garlic, dry-roasted (see page 116)

3 to 5 serrano chiles, fire-roasted but not peeled (see pages 18–19)

¹/₂ cup olive oil

³/₄ teaspoon salt

¹/₄ teaspoon ground pepper

Juice of 1 lime

Put all ingredients in a blender or food processor and purée until smooth. If making the marinade ahead, don't add the lime juice until just before using in order to retain the vibrant green color.

Pour over meats, poultry, or seafood in a shallow nonreactive pan, cover, and refrigerate. Marinate poultry for 2 to 3 hours, pork for 4 to 6 hours, and swordfish, scallops, or shrimp for 1 to 2 hours.

canela brine

makes about 4 cups

This brine is ideal for pork, quail, lamb, and even chicken. Since the taste of cinnamon is a natural for the rustic flavors of grilling, this also makes a great marinade for meats that aren't going near the smokehouse. Just enough sodium nitrate is called for to maintain the colors of the food, and your meats won't take on unnatural colors or become ham-like. Dextrose, a granulated form of glucose, is a sugar that will offset the firming effect of the salts and take a little of the harsh edge off of the smoke. If you can't locate curing salts in your area, the Sausagemaker, in Buffalo, New York, is a great source for spices and supplies for the home sausage maker (see Mail-Order Sources). See pages 54–55 for information on range-top smoking.

4 cups water

1 $^1/_2$ tablespoons kosher salt

3 tablespoons canela, or 1 $^1/_2$ tablespoons ground
  cinnamon

2 $^1/_2$ teaspoons sodium nitrate

2 $^1/_2$ teaspoons dextrose

Bring the water to a boil in a medium saucepan. Turn off the heat and stir in all the remaining ingredients until dissolved. Cover the brine and refrigerate it for at least 2 hours, or until completely chilled. Soak smaller pieces of meat, such as quail, for 1 to 2 hours, and larger pieces, such as racks of lamb and whole chickens, for no more than 3 hours. Such larger pieces will be best if hot-smoked, then finished in the oven or on a rotisserie the next day, after the flavors have had a chance to meld.

NOTE: Cinnamon and canela will give brine a viscous, almost oily, feeling that in no way connotes unwholesomeness.

jay's quick and easy barbecue sauce

makes about 4 cups

Several of the recipes in this book call for barbecue sauce as an ingredient. Jay Comfort, a Washington-area chef who helped in the development of many of these recipes, came up with this one, and it is definitely true to its name. The chipotles bring a hint of smokiness to foods that haven't yet been anywhere near a grill or smokehouse.

1 tablespoon olive oil

2 cups sliced onions

1 $^1/_2$ cups cider vinegar

2 ancho chiles and 6 chipotle chiles, stemmed,
  seeded, and toasted (see page 24)

10 large cloves garlic, roasted (see page 116)

1 cup molasses or to taste

2 $^1/_2$ cups ketchup

About $^1/_2$ cup water

Salt to taste

In a large sauté pan or skillet over medium-high heat, heat the olive oil and sauté the onions until they are browned and completely soft, about 2 to 3 minutes. Add the vinegar and bring it to a simmer. Add the chiles to the pan along with the garlic, molasses, and ketchup and stir well to blend. Simmer for 5 to 8 minutes or until the flavors are blended. Add some or all of the water to adjust the consistency. Put the sauce into a blender and purée it until smooth. Strain the sauce through a coarse-meshed sieve. Store in an airtight container in the refrigerator for up to 8 days.

red sage pork and chicken chorizo

makes 4 1/2 pounds bulk sausage

In this recipe from the Red Sage restaurant, lean chicken and nonfat dried milk replace a substantial amount of the fat found in most chorizos. As a result, this sausage is very lean but flavorful, and doesn't weep a red-chile residue onto other foods as some chorizos do. Adding ice keeps the sausage chilled and adds moisture so that it won't brown before it is completely cooked.

2 pounds boneless pork butt, cut into 1-inch cubes

1 pound boneless, skinless chicken breast, cut into cubes

1 pound unsalted fatback, cut into 1-inch cubes

1 bunch fresh cilantro, stemmed and chopped

3/4 tablespoon chile molido

1/4 cup paprika

1 1/2 tablespoons cayenne pepper

2 1/2 teaspoons ground cumin

1 teaspoon ground cinnamon

1/2 teaspoon garlic powder

Pinch of ground cloves

5 teaspoons salt

5 teaspoons nonfat dried milk

1 1/4 cups crushed ice

Grind the pork, chicken, fatback, and cilantro in a meat grinder fitted with the 1/4-inch grinding plate. Add all the spices, the salt, and dried milk. Place the sausage in the bowl of an electric mixer (if using a heavy-duty mixer, use the paddle attachment). Mix for 1 minute at low speed while adding the ice in small increments. Mix for 1 minute at medium speed. The sausage may be used in bulk form or formed into patties. It may also be piped into casings and tied into links.

chicken stock

makes 8 cups

This good all-purpose chicken stock can be used for any of the recipes in this book that call for it.

4 pounds chicken bones, from about 3 large birds

12 cups water

1 carrot, diced

1 onion, halved

4 stalks celery, diced

1 bay leaf

1 sprig fresh thyme, or 1 pinch dried thyme

3 peppercorns, crushed

2 to 3 parsley stems

Rinse the bones in cold water and cut them into 3- to 4-inch pieces with a cleaver or heavy knife. Put them in a stockpot with the water. Bring the water to a boil, then reduce the heat to a slow simmer. Using a large spoon, skim off the film that rises to the surface. Add the vegetables and herbs and continue to simmer, uncovered, for 5 to 6 hours, occasionally skimming off the fat or foam. Add water as needed to keep the bones just covered.

Strain the stock and let it cool to room temperature. Store, covered, up to 3 days in the refrigerator, or up to 3 months in the freezer. If fat has congealed on the surface of the stock, lift it off after the stock is cold and discard.

brown duck stock

makes about 8 cups

In pipiáns and moles, duck stock can add a richer, more intense flavor than chicken stock or water. Any fat left over from roasting the bones can be reserved for the frying step.

4 pounds duck bones, from 2 to 3 large birds

12 cups water

1 onion, halved

1 carrot, sliced

$^1/_2$ stalk celery, sliced

2 garlic cloves, crushed

1 bay leaf

1 sprig fresh thyme, or 1 pinch dry thyme

4 peppercorns, crushed

3 to 4 parsley stems

4 to 5 tablespoons tomato purée

Preheat the oven to 375°. Rinse the bones in cold water and cut them into 3- to 4-inch pieces with a cleaver or large knife. Put the bones one layer deep in a roasting pan and roast them in the oven, stirring occasionally, for 20 to 40 minutes, or until they are brown.

Drain off and reserve the fat and transfer the bones to a stockpot. Add 1 cup of the water to the roasting pan and stir it over medium heat to scrape up the browned bits from the bottom of the pan. Add this mixture to the stock pot. Add the remaining water and bring to a simmer.

In a medium sauté pan or skillet over medium heat, heat 1 tablespoon of the reserved duck fat and sauté the onion, carrot, celery, and garlic for 6 to 8 minutes, or until evenly browned. Drain this mixture well and add it to the simmering stock with the bay leaf, thyme, peppercorns, parsley stems, and tomato purée.

Return the stock to a simmer and cook for 5 to 6 hours, occasionally skimming off the foam. Add water as necessary to keep all ingredients just covered.

Strain the stock and spoon off any fat from the surface. Store, covered, in the refrigerator for up to 3 days, or freeze for up to 3 months. If any fat has coagulated on the surface of the cold stock, lift it off and reserve it for other uses or discard.

words you should know

ne thing that keeps people out of the Southwestern kitchen is the language barrier. Words such as *escabeche* and *pipián* are becoming more familiar, though, and will soon undoubtedly become part of our daily vernacular, as the terms *beurre blanc* and *beárnaise* did a generation or so ago. The following list includes words used in this book, and many more that are included in other southwestern and Mexican cookbooks.

achiote paste see page 7

adobo A vinegary red sauce either made with or used to preserve chiles, adobo may also be used for pickling. Food that is prepared and served in this sauce is said to be served *en adobo*.

albóndigas *(ahl-BOHN-dee-gahs)* Small meatballs made of chicken, shrimp, beef, or pork and usually used as a garnish for broth soups or served in tomato sauce as an appetizer or light entrée.

aniseed These crescent-shaped seeds are a member of the parsley family. Used in both sweet and savory dishes, they impart a strong licorice flavor and a lightly sweet tone to food, and provide a welcome counterpoint to the flavor of chiles.

annatto seeds see page 7

atole *(a-TOH-lay)* An ancient beverage made by boiling ground dry-roasted corn and water. This is the traditional drink served with tamales. Atoles may be flavored with chocolate, nuts, or cinnamon and other spices and sweetened with sugar for a hearty breakfast drink. They are sometimes blended with chiles to make a savory porridge-like dish.

bolillos *(boh-LEE-ohs)* Small hard rolls with a texture and crust similar to French rolls.

buckwheat This deceptively named plant is not a grain, but an herb whose seeds bring a distinctive nutty, slightly fermented flavor to pancakes and other baked goods, as well as to pasta and noodles. Because buckwheat has a naturally low gluten content, it is mixed with other flours in baking.

cabrito *(kah-BREE-toh)* Young, or kid, goat, which is usually split and spit roasted whole. This dish is a favorite in northern Mexico, especially at Easter.

cactus The pads and fruits of the *Opuntia* cactus are cooked and consumed. Cactus pads and prickly pear fruit are illustrated and discussed on pages 10–11.

cajeta *(ka-HEH-tah)* A thick, rich sweet, usually made from goat's milk and cinnamon. (See also page 108)

canela see page 7

carnitas *(kar-NEE-tahs)* Chunks of pork that have been seasoned, slow-cooked, and seared in their own fat. In Mexican cooking, this is a traditional taco and enchilada filling.

chalupas *(cha-LOU-pahs)* Corn or flour tortillas that have been fried into a basket shape for filling with meat fillings and/or salads.

chayote see page 9

cherimoya see page 10

chicos *(CHEE-kohs)* Whole kernels of dried corn. Unlike pozole, which has been treated with slaked lime, chicos still have their tough outer skins. These may be cooked for hours to serve as a vegetable, or ground into *harinella*, which may be used interchangeably with *masa harina*.

chiles, dried see also pages 5–6

cayenne *(KI-anne)* Also known as **ginnie peppers**, cayennes are 3 to 8 inches long and slender, measuring about ¹/₂ inch across. These fiery small chiles have a very direct and alert flavor. Cayennes can be used in soups and stews, but are most commonly ground and used as a seasoning. **Chiles de árbol** (see page 6) are closely related to cayennes and can be substituted in a pinch.

habaneros *(ah-bah-NARE-ohs)* Dried habaneros have a very thin flesh and an intense tropical flavor. They have tones of coconut and papaya, and are so hot that their use is limited to the very heartiest soups, sauces, and stews. They are also deseeded and ground into a powder for use as a powerful seasoning.

mora *(MO-rah)* A more subtle variety of the smoked jalapeño than chipotles, moras have a long mesquite flavor with tones of dried fruit. *Moras grandes* are a larger version of the same type of chile, while smaller ones are often labeled *moritas*. Use **chipotles** (see page 6) as a substitute for any of these chiles.

mulato *(moo-LAH-toh)* A very dark broad chile that tastes of licorice, chocolate, and dried fruit, mulatos are used in many dark moles. Since their flavor is not as deep and full as some other dried chiles, they are often blended with heartier types in sauces and stews. If unavailable, use **anchos** (see page 5) or **pasillas**.

pasilla *(pah-SEE-ah)* The word *pasilla* means "little raisin" and refers to their raisin color and texture and their hint of grape flavor. The pasilla is a member of the "holy trinity" of chiles that includes the **ancho** and the **mulato**. These three chiles blended together form the base of many traditional moles. Pasillas are thin fleshed, with flavors of dried fruit and licorice. Substitute **anchos** (see page 5) if these are not available.

pequín *(pe-KEEN)* Small potent dried chiles that were used by the Native Americans to preserve meats. These chiles have a light orange color and oval shape. Their thin flesh has sweet tones of corn and smoke, with a touch of citrus. Pequíns are used in salsas, soups, and sauces. Use **tepíns** if these are unavailable.

tepín *(teh-PEEN)* A wild form of the pequín, this little fireball grows along the Mexican and U.S. border and throughout the Caribbean. Tepíns are round, measure about ¹/₂ inch across, and have a searing, dry heat. They are used in sauces, stews, and salsas. Substitute **pequíns** if these chiles are unavailable.

chiles, fresh see also pages 3–4.

cubanelle *(que-BAH-nell)* A mild and slightly sweet light green to yellow chile. Measuring 4 to 5 inches long, the cubanelle is one of the most commonly available chiles on the eastern seaboard. It is good for roasting and cutting into *rajas*, dicing and using raw in colorful salsas and pickling for escabeches. If unavailable, **Anaheims** (see page 3) may be substituted.

Fresno Very similar in size and appearance to a ripe jalapeño, these bright red chiles are broader at the shoulders and considerably hotter. Thick-fleshed Fresnos are great in salsas and ceviches and are usually available only in the fall. If unavailable, use ripe **jalapeños** (see page 3).

güero *(WHARE-oh)* The word means "blond" or "light skinned" in Spanish, and is a generic term applied to a variety of yellow chiles. Most often, güero refers to long tapered varieties such as banana peppers, Hungarian wax chiles, and Santa Fe grandes. They all tend to be mildly sweet to slightly hot, with a waxy but tart texture. Güeros are used in yellow moles, salads and salsas, and escabeches.

Hatch A close relative of the **New Mexico green** chile (see page 3).

New Mexico red In the autumn, a large portion of the New Mexico chile crop is left on the vine to ripen. Much of the crop is strung into ristras for drying, but some are marketed fresh. As with most ripe chiles, they are mellower and sweeter than their green counterparts. They are used in pipiáns, barbecue sauces, and salsas.

pimiento When the chile made its way to the Old World via Columbus, the timid palates of the Europeans prompted them to breed larger, sweeter varieties. The pimiento is one of the better results of that labor. Meaty and luscious, with just a tinge of spice, this chile is grown in Spain, Hungary, California, and the southern United States. When dried, pimientos are ground into paprika. Use fresh red bell peppers if pimientos are unavailable.

chorizo *(chor-EE-zoh)* A spicy pork sausage flavored with garlic and chile molido. Mexican chorizo is sold fresh and is often cooked to add to fillings and egg dishes. Spanish chorizo, a hard sausage that is dried and smoked in casings, is somewhat milder in both flavor and heat.

cilantro see page 7

coriander see page 8

corn husks The dried outer leaves of corn "ears." These husks are the traditional and most common wrapper for tamales and for wrapping fish to be steamed. Beware of worm holes and dark or discolored spots when purchasing dried husks. They will keep indefinitely, but should be used within a day or two of being rehydrated. You can make your own dried corn husks by allowing fresh husks to air-dry for 2 to 3 days. Corn husks can also be used fresh for many tamale recipes. Tamales and fish can also be wrapped in banana leaves for a more tropical flavor and appearance.

crema see page 101

epazote see page 8

escabeche see page 37

frijoles *(free-HO-lays)* Beans. One of the native American plants originally cultivated by the Indians, beans were a primary staple of the diets of both Native Americans and pioneers. Rare heirloom varieties and new hybrids seem to appear on grocery shelves almost daily. Following are descriptions of the types most often called for in southwestern recipes. Methods for soaking and cooking beans are discussed on pages 117–118.

Anasazi Named after "the ancient ones," ancestors of the southwestern Native Americans, this is one of the oldest bean cultivars. Developed by the forebears of the Pueblo Indians in what is now New Mexico, these beans have a variegated cranberry-and-white coloring that adds color to bean dishes and side salads.

black turtle Also known as *frijoles negros* or black beans, this native of the Yucatán is probably the most common bean used in southwestern cooking. Satiny black on the exterior, they are creamy white inside, with a hearty, almost smoky flavor. Commonly used in soups and low-fat sauces, as well as in side dishes, the cooked beans can also be rinsed and added to salsas for visual interest.

bollito This ancestor of the **pinto** bean is more compact and flavorful, and takes quite a bit longer to cook. The bollito is often used in the broth-style side dishes of Mexican cuisine.

pinto The name, taken from *pintar*, "to paint," refers to the splotchy reddish-brown skins of these beans, which turn pink when cooked. Their mild flavor cries out for toasted spices, bacon or ham trimmings, and grassy herbs such as marjoram or Mexican oregano. When a recipe title simply says *frijoles*, it is most likely referring to pintos.

red Euphemistically referred to as "the Mexican strawberry" in the Southwest, this bean is brighter in color than the **pinto** and lacks the surface streaks of its slightly smaller relative. Red beans are similar in taste to pintos, and they are often used interchangeably.

guava A sweet, fragrant tropical fruit that is native to Peru and Brazil and is now grown in Florida, Hawaii, and California. Guava has a bright yellow to hot pink flesh and the fruit may be quite sour unless it is fully ripe, which it will be when heavy for its size and slightly soft. A preponderance of pithy seeds make the guava best suited for sorbets, beverages, and sauces.

harinella *(ah-ree-NE-lah)* See *chicos*.

hierba santa see page 8

hibiscus The blossoms of this tropical plant provide a brilliant color and an intense blackberry and dried cherry flavor to cocktails, marinades, and vinaigrettes. Hibiscus can be purchased in most Latino markets.

Ibarra chocolate The traditional Mexican chocolate, which contains cinnamon, ground almonds, and sugar, Ibarra is the modern version of an Aztec chocolate drink that sometimes contained chiles. It is ideal for making hot chocolate, but should not be substituted for regular chocolate in most other recipes.

marjoram A member of the mint family, marjoram is very similar in taste to oregano, but is milder and sweeter. Often labeled as **sweet marjoram**, it is used to season pork and game. Because it is more floral and delicate than oregano, marjoram is often preferred in many dishes.

masa *(MAH-sah)* The word *masa* means dough, and refers to corn-based dough used for traditional tortillas and tamales. Fresh masa is made from corn kernels that have been either sun- or fire-dried, then boiled in water and lime (calcium oxide). After being soaked overnight in their cooking water, the kernels are ground into masa.

masa harina *(MAH-sah ah-REE-nah)* Uncooked corn kernels that have been ground into flour. (The name means "dough flour.") Used to make tortilla and tamales. Available in Latino and other markets.

menudo *(meh-NOO-dough)* A robust and hearty soup made with tripe, calves' feet, and posole, notorious for its use as a hangover curative. A traditional Mexican dish for New Year's Day, menudo is usually served with lime wedges and hot tortillas.

Mexican oregano Possessing much larger leaves and a very different appearance from the oregano most commonly found in the United States, Mexican oregano is almost always sold dried in this country. A member of the same verbena family as Greek or common oregano, this variegated plant is more pungent and has a slightly "wilder" taste. Many traditional recipes for red sauces, moles, and stews call for this herb, and it is available in most Latino markets and many specialty foods stores. As with most dried spices, Mexican oregano should be toasted slightly before using.

mole *(MOH-lay)* Possibly one of the oldest known sauces, the name is taken from the Nahuatl word *molli*, meaning "concoction." The best-known moles in America are flavored with chocolate, though most moles are not.

natilla *(nah-TEE-yah)* A very sweet dessert of meringue poached and served in custard sauce. Very similar to the classic floating islands, it is often accompanied with fresh or poached fruits.

nopales see page 10

nopalitos *(noh-pah-LEE-tohs)* Nopales that have been cut into strips or dices. Usually refers to the canned and pickled cactus.

Panko *(PAN-ko)* Also known as **Japanese breadcrumbs**, these coarse dry white breadcrumbs are great to use for breading rellenos and other fried foods. Similar to untoasted coconut in appearance, they provide a nuttier, crisper crust than regular breadcrumbs. Panko is found in Asian markets and many grocery stores. If necessary, substitute plain white breadcrumbs.

pepitas see page 10

piloncillo *(pee-lon-SEE-oh)* Unrefined sugar sold in small solid cones. Piloncillo has a unique rustic flavor, but if it is unavailable, brown sugar may be substituted.

piñons see page 11

posole see page 13

prickly pear see page 11

queso *(KAY-soh)* Cheese. Many southwestern recipes call for fresh Mexican cheeses, which are becoming increasingly available. Where possible, substitutions are noted.

queso añejo A salty white cheese that is slightly similar to feta in flavor. As añejo is not brined, its flavor is somewhat milder.

queso asadero *(KAY-so ah-sah-DARE-oh)* Also known as **quesilla de Oaxaca**. A rubbery-textured cheese that is pulled and twisted into strands. This cheese is traditionally used in fillings, where, like mozzarella, it becomes stringy when heated. Whole-milk mozzarella, Monterey jack, or Muenster may be substituted.

queso fresco *(KAY-so fres-KHO)* A crumbly white cheese made from partially skimmed milk, queso fresco is lightly tangy and very subtle. It is usually sold in small round cakes and is used for fillings and crumbled into soups and over sauces. In a pinch, try substituting a mild feta, though it will still be a good bit stronger in flavor. Fresh farmer's cheese, if available, is a better replacement.

manchego An aged sheep's milk cheese that is dry and crumbly. This cheese is packed in straw and weighted, and is usually grated for use in quesadillas and empanadas. If it is unavailable, substitute a good Parmesan or aged white Cheddar.

rajas *(rah-HAHS)* Chiles or bell peppers that have been cut into thin strips. Usually the chiles and peppers will have been roasted and peeled before being cut into julienne.

ristra *(rees-TRAH)* A string of chiles for drying in the sun. The dry mountain air around Santa Fe is ideal for this, and long strands of bright New Mexico reds color the rafters and awnings of homes and barns there in late summer and early autumn.

squash blossoms The male flowers of several varieties of squash, most commonly zucchini and yellow squash. They may be cooked briefly for use in soups or sauces, or stuffed and fried.

star anise Although botanically unrelated to aniseed, this star-shaped pod has a similar but stronger flavor and more fragrant perfume. It is most often cooked whole and strained from sauces and marinades, but is sometimes ground for spice rubs and pastes.

streaker Although the word usually refers to bean purées or other colorful pastes made from nondairy products and used to decorate plates and finished dishes, it may also refer to brightly colored cremas.

tamarind see page 12

vanilla The dark, thin seed pods of a perennial orchid that was originally cultivated in Mexico. Used primarily to flavor desserts and beverages.

yuca *(YOU-kah)* Also known as **cassava**, this dark-skinned root has a soft white flesh. Yuca is cooked and mashed for side dishes, sweetened and fried for desserts, or cooked into soups and stews to serve as a thickener. Yuca can also be thinly sliced and fried into chips, and it is the base from which tapioca is made.

some notes on measurements and conversions

Recipes in some books will call for half a cup of diced peppers or 3 tablespoons of lime juice, and so on, without giving per-piece shopping guidelines. Accepting as we must that an "ear of corn" or a "bunch of cilantro" are not standard units of measure, the following approximate equivalents are offered.

cheese	1 cup grated (most types)	2 ounces
	1 cup diced or crumbled	5 ounces
chiles	1 medium bell pepper, seeded and diced	1/2 cup
	1 medium bell pepper, roasted, peeled, seeded and diced	7 tablespoons or a scant 1/2 cup
	1 large jalapeño, diced with seeds	4 teaspoons
	1 large jalapeño, diced without seeds	1 tablespoon
	1 large serrano, diced with seeds	1 tablespoon
	1 medium serrano, diced with seeds	2 teaspoons
citrus	juice of 1 medium orange	1/4 cup
	juice of 1 medium lime	5 teaspoons
	juice of 1 medium lemon	7 teaspoons
corn	1 large ear	1 cup kernels
	1 medium ear	3/4 cup kernels
eggs (grade A large)	eggs per cup	5
	whites per cup	7
	yolks per cup	12
herbs	1 bunch basil or cilantro leaves	1 cup
	1 cup whole basil or cilantro leaves	1/2 cup chopped
lettuces	1 cup	1 ounce
nuts & seeds	1 cup	4 ounces
onion	1 medium	2 cups peeled and diced

conversion charts

Volume formulas:

1 teaspoon = 4.93 mL

1 tablespoon = 14.79 mL/3 teaspoons

1 cup = 236.59 mL/16 tablespoons

1 L = 202.88 teaspoons/67.63 tablespoons/4.23 cups

1/4 cup	59 mL
1/3 cup	78 mL
1/2 cup	118 mL
2/3 cup	159 mL
3/4 cup	177 mL
1 cup	237 mL
2 cups	473 mL
3 cups	710 mL
4 cups	946 mL
5 cups	1.2 L
6 cups	1.4 L
7 cups	1.7 L
8 cups	1.9 L
9 cups	2 L

1/2 tablespoon	7 mL
1 tablespoon	15 mL
1 1/2 tablespoon	22 mL
2 tablespoons	30 mL
3 tablespoons	44 mL
4 tablespoons (1/4 cup)	59 mL
5 tablespoons	74 mL
6 tablespoons	89 mL
7 tablespoons	104 mL
8 tablespoons (1/2 cup)	118 mL
9 tablespoons	133 mL
10 tablespoons	148 mL
11 tablespoons	163 mL
12 tablespoons (3/4 cup)	177 mL
13 tablespoons	192 mL
14 tablespoons	207 mL
15 tablespoons	222 mL

1 teaspoon	5 mL
2 teaspoons	10 mL
3 teaspoons (1 tablespoon)	15 mL
4 teaspoons	20 mL
5 teaspoons	25 mL
6 teaspoons (2 tablespoons)	30 mL
8 teaspoons	39 mL
9 teaspoons	44 mL
10 teaspoons	49 mL

length formulas

1 inch = 2.54 cm

1 foot = .3 m/12 inches

1 cm = .39 inch

1 m = 3.28 feet/39.37 inches

1/4 inch	.6 cm	5 inches	13 cm
1/2 inch	1 cm	6 inches (1/2 foot)	15 cm
3/4 inch	2 cm	7 inches	18 cm
1 inch	2.5 cm	8 inches	20 cm
1 1/2 inches	4 cm	9 inches	23 cm
2 inches	5 cm	10 inches	25 cm
2 1/2 inches	6 cm	11 inches	28 cm
3 inches	8 cm	12 inches (1 foot)	30 cm
3 1/2 inches	9 cm	18 inches (1 and 1/2 foot)	46 cm
4 inches	10 cm		

temperature formulas

$9/5 \, C + 32 = F$

$(F - 32) \times 5/9 = C$

275°F	135°C/gas mark 1
300°F	149°C/gas mark 2
325°F	163°C/gas mark 3
350°F	177°C/gas mark 4
375°F	191°C/gas mark 5
400°F	204°C/gas mark 6
425°F	218°C/gas mark 7
450°F	232°C/gas mark 8
475°F	246°C/gas mark 9
500°F	260°C

weight

1 ounce = 28.35 g

1 pound = 453.59 g/16 ounces

1 kg = 2.2 pounds

1/2 ounce	14 g	10 1/2 ounces	298 g
1 ounce	28 g	11 ounces	312 g
1 1/2 ounces	43 g	11 1/2 ounces	326 g
2 ounces	57 g	12 ounces	340 g
2 1/2 ounces	71 g	12 1/2 ounces	354 g
3 ounces	85 g	13 ounces	369 g
3 1/2 ounces	100 g	13 1/2 ounces	383 g
4 ounces (1/4 pound)	113 g	14 ounces	397 g
4 1/2 ounces	128 g	14 1/2 ounces	411 g
5 ounces	142 g	15 ounces	425 g
5 1/2 ounces	156 g	15 1/2 ounces	439 g
6 ounces	170 g	16 ounces (1 pound)	454 g
6 1/2 ounces	184 g	1 1/2 pounds	680 g
7 ounces	198 g	2 pounds	907 g
7 1/2 ounces	213 g	2 1/2 pounds	1.1 kg
8 ounces (1/2 pound)	227 g	3 pounds	1.4 kg
8 1/2 ounces	241 g	3 1/2 pounds	1.6 kg
9 ounces	255 g	4 pounds	1.8 kg
9 1/2 ounces	270 g	4 1/2 pounds	2 kg
10 ounces	283 g		

mail-order sources

Coyote Cafe General Store
132 West Water Street
Santa Fe, NM 87501
(800) 866-HOWL or
(505) 982-2454
Beans, chiles (including canned chipotles en adobo), canela, spices,
tamarind, Coyote Cocina Howlin' Hot Sauce.

Elizabeth Berry
Gallina Canyon Ranch
144 Camino Escondido
Santa Fe, NM 87501
(505) 982-4149
Beans and specialty produce.

Bueno Foods
2001 4th Street S.W.
Albuquerque, NM 87102
(505) 243-2722
Chiles, hoja santa, epazote.

Glen Burns
16158 Hillside Circle
Montverde, FL 34756
(407) 469-4490
Huitlacoche.

Dean and Deluca
560 Broadway
New York, NY 10012
(212) 431-1691
Chiles, oils, vinegars, beans.

The Sausagemaker
26 Military Road
Buffalo, NY 14207
(716) 876-5521
Sausage- and brine-making supplies, fine hickory chips.

Del Valle Pecans
P.O. Box 104
Mesilla Park, NM 88047
(505) 524-1867
Organic pecans.

Luhr Jensen & Sons, Inc.
P.O. Box 297
Hood River, OR 97031
(503) 386-3811
Alder, apple, cherry, and hickory chips.

Williams-Sonoma
P.O. Box 7456
San Francisco, CA 94120-7456
(800) 541-2233
Kitchen tools and gadgets and specialty foods.

index